How to Pass

FCE

First Certificate in English

Exam practice in
Use of English

PAPER THREE

Brian Orpet

Contents

1	**INTRODUCTION**	**1**
2	**PART 1: MULTIPLE CHOICE CLOZE**	**3**
	Looking at Part 1	3
	The missing words	3
	Filling in the answer sheet	3
	Choosing the missing words	4
	Words which are tested	4
	Practice exercises	5
	Doing the exam	7
	Exam exercises	8
3	**PART 2: OPEN CLOZE**	**12**
	Looking at Part 2	12
	The missing words	12
	Filling in the answer sheet	12
	Words which are tested	12
	Practice exercises	13
	Doing the exam	15
	Exam exercises	16
4	**PART 3: TRANSFORMATIONS**	**18**
	Looking at Part 3	18
	Filling in the answer sheet	18
	Deciding on the missing words	18
	Doing the exam	20
	Exam exercises	20
5	**PART 4: ERROR CORRECTION**	**26**
	Looking at the exam	26
	Mistakes and correct lines	26
	How to do the exam	26
	Filling in the answer sheet	27
	Some extra words to look for	27
	Practice exercises	28
	Doing the exam	29
	Exam exercises	30
6	**PART 5: WORD FORMATION**	**33**
	Looking at the exam	33
	Filling in the answer sheet	33
	Words to be formed	33
	Reading the passage	34
	Plurals	35
	Negatives	35
	Practice exercises	36
	Doing the exam	37
	Exam exercises	38
	TRIAL PAPER A	**40**
	TRIAL PAPER B	**45**
	ANSWERS AND NOTES	**50**
	APPENDIX	**67**
	ANSWER SHEETS	**70**

This book is for students who are preparing on their own for the new (1996) Cambridge First Certificate Examination in English and also for students in schools or colleges who wish to have extra practice material.

The book explains what the five parts of Paper 3 Use of English consist of and gives suggestions on what types of question may be asked and how candidates should approach the different parts of this paper.

There are two kinds of exercise:
- **Practice Exercises** are shorter and easier than in the First Certificate, and build up the necessary skills.
- **Exam Exercises** are at the level of First Certificate, and the same length as in the exam.

There are also two full **Trial Papers** at the end of the book.

Answers to all the exercises and trial papers, sometimes with notes to explain answers, are given in the **Answers and Notes** section on page 50.

The book will help students to become familiar with Paper 3 and will give them confidence in taking the examination. It should, however, be made clear that this is *not* a grammar course book.

USING THE BOOK

Different students will find different ways of using the book.

Most students will benefit from studying each part of the book in order and doing two of the four Exam Exercises in each part. When students have completed all five parts, they should try to do the remaining Exam Exercises in each part and, finally, the two full Trial Papers.

Some students who feel confident in one or two parts of the paper may ignore those parts and concentrate on the other parts. Other students may wish to work simply on the exercises and to ignore the explanations in each part.

TRIAL PAPERS

The two full papers are called Trial Papers. To gain full value from these, students should work through them under examination conditions – that is, taking the correct length of time for the paper and not referring to any books whilst doing it. There are two answer sheets at the back of the book which students may use to write their answers as they would in the actual examination.

As the Exam Exercises in the different parts of the book are all of First Certificate level, students may, if they wish, make up extra Trial Papers by putting together Exam Exercises from the five different parts of the book.

Before doing the Trial Papers it is a good idea to look at the section for each part of Paper 3 called **Doing the exam** and **Remember**.

APPENDIX

The appendix at the back of the book is a list of words to help you understand grammar terms which are used in the book. All through the book, you will see that certain words are followed by an asterisk (*). The asterisk means that the word indicated appears in the appendix.

MARKS

In all parts except part 3, every answer is worth 1 mark. In part 3 every answer is worth 2 marks. This means that the total mark for the paper is 75.

Pass Mark

All five papers in the First Certificate carry the same final mark, even though the number of questions is not the same. That is, each of the 5 papers carries 20% of the total mark. In order to pass the First Certificate, you need to reach a total mark of about 60% across the five papers – that is, a mark of 45 out of 75 on Paper 3. In theory, you could fail one of the papers and still pass the whole exam, but you would have to do extremely well in all the other papers.

TIME

You will have 1 hour and 15 minutes to do this paper. Generally, it is best to work through the paper in the order of the parts (that is Part 1 first, Part 2 second, and so on). However, if you have always found one part far more difficult than the other parts, it may be a good idea to leave this until the end.

When you do the Trial Papers, you should get an idea of how long to spend on the different parts of the paper. Below is a suggestion on how long to spend on these parts:

Part 1:   15 minutes
Part 2:   10 minutes
Part 3:   15 minutes
Part 4:   15 minutes
Part 5:   10 minutes
Revision: 10 minutes

Remember these times are *only suggestions* and they will not be suitable for everyone. You may well spend more time on parts which you find difficult and less time on parts you find easy. Doing the Trial Papers should help you to organise your time in the most suitable way for yourself.

PENCIL AND RUBBER

In the examination, all answers must be written on the answer sheet in pencil. The centre where you are taking the examination may provide you with a pencil for the test but it is a good idea to take a pencil of your own in case the centre does not give you one. It is also sensible to take a rubber with you to rub out any answers which you wish to change.

LOOKING AT PART 1

In this part of the Use of English paper, you have a passage to read in which there are sixteen empty spaces where words are missing. After the passage, for each empty space there is a choice of four words which could be used to fill the space. You must choose which one of these words is the most suitable.

It is very important to note that the first empty space is an example and always has the number **0**. You will find the choice of words to fill this empty space and the correct answer above the title of the passage. Be careful not to put the answer for **0** as your first answer – remember this is an example which has been done for you.

THE MISSING WORDS

The missing words will usually test your knowledge of vocabulary rather than your ability to use grammar correctly.

Although the choice for filling the empty spaces will usually consist of four single words, occasionally the choice will consist of four short phrases of two or three words each. These will usually be *compound prepositions** or *phrasal verbs**. Here are two examples of this type of choice:

A instead of	**B** in case	**C** owing to	**D** if only
A give away	**B** take back	**C** get off	**D** look for

Occasionally two words may be used to allow you to have a choice between two words beginning with a vowel* and two with a consonant*. Here is an example:

A an appointment	**B** a time	**C** an interview	**D** a date

FILLING IN THE ANSWER SHEET

In front of each of these four words is a letter (**A**, **B**, **C** or **D**). When you have chosen the word which you think is most suitable, you do not write the word down but you put a mark in pencil on the answer sheet (see page 70) under the letter which has been used to indicate this word. Imagine that part of the passage had this sentence in it.

John put his **(6)** .... on as he saw that it was raining.

In the choice of words after the passage these four words are suggested as possible for filling empty space number 6:

6   **A** tie   **B** raincoat   **C** socks   **D** shirt

The correct answer is **B** (raincoat) so you put a mark in the little box under the letter B on your answer sheet, as shown below.

CHOOSING THE MISSING WORDS

When you read through the passage, you may feel that you know what the missing word is before you even look at the choice of words which you are given. When you then look at the choice of words and immediately see that the word you had thought of is there, do not just choose that answer without looking at the other words given; it may well be that the word you thought of is not the most suitable one to fill the empty space.

Read through the choice of words, decide which words are not suitable to fill the empty space and, finally, choose the word which you think is most suitable.

As mentioned above, each of the words has a letter in front of it (**A**, **B**, **C** or **D**). Do not choose an answer by thinking that because one of these letters has not yet been used for a correct answer, it must be the letter which will indicate the next correct answer. If you are, for example, at question 8 and C has never been the correct answer, do not think that C must now be the correct answer. In the same way, if one letter has often indicated the correct answer, do not think that it cannot again indicate a correct answer. If, for example, you are on question 9 and letter D has already been the correct answer on six occasions, do not think that it cannot indicate the correct answer again. The main reason for this is that you may have made a mistake in some of the earlier answers when the letter D was not in fact the correct answer. (If they wanted to do so, examiners could use A as the correct answer for every empty space or could decide never to use B for a correct answer, though, in reality, this would never happen.)

The only time when it is acceptable to decide on which letter to choose by looking at the letters that have already been used is when you have no idea at all what the answer is. If this happens, then you might make a choice by looking at which letters have not been used. You should **always** make sure that you give an answer, even if it is not much more than a guess.

WORDS WHICH ARE TESTED

Almost any word can be tested in this part of the paper. The words to fill the empty spaces may be nouns*, verbs*, adjectives*, adverbs*, prepositions*, etc. You will often find phrasal verbs* being tested here (e.g. *set off, put on*) and set expressions (e.g. *take place, pay attention*).

Five sets of words which are likely to be tested fairly often are the following:

Arrive/reach/get
Arrive must normally be followed by *at*, *get* must be followed by *to*, but *reach* is not followed by any preposition*. Note the following examples:

    Peter finally *arrived at* his destination.
    Peter finally *got to* his destination.
    Peter finally r*eached* his destination.

(An exception to the above is the word *home*, as *at* and *to* are never used with *home*: *arrive home, get home, reach home*.)

Manage/succeed
Manage is followed by *to* + verb*. *Succeed* is followed by *in* + verb ending in *-ing*. Note the following examples:

    I finally *managed to open* the door.
    I finally *succeeded in opening* the door.

Allow/permit/let
Allow and *permit* are both followed by a noun* (or pronoun*) and a verb* with *to* in front of the verb. *Let* is followed by a noun or pronoun and a verb without *to*. Note the following examples:

    The police *allowed* my friend *to enter* the building.
    The police *let* my friend *enter* the building.

Cause/force/make

Cause when it means 'to force somebody (or something) to do something' is followed by a noun* (or pronoun*) and a verb* with *to* in front of the verb. *Make* is followed by a noun or pronoun and a verb without *to*. Note the following examples:

The hot weather *caused* him *to lose* his temper.

The hot weather *made* him *lose* his temper.

Continue/carry/keep

These three verbs* can all have the meaning 'continue'. However *carry* and *keep* must both be followed by *on* and the *-ing* form of the verb. *Continue* must be followed either by the *-ing* form of the verb or *to* and the verb. Note the following examples:

They *carried on singing.*

They *kept on singing.*

They *continued singing.*

They *continued to sing.*

PRACTICE EXERCISES

Below are ten Practice Exercises for you to work through before beginning the full Exam Exercises. These Practice Exercises are far shorter than the Exam Exercises and also rather easier. They will help you to get used to doing this sort of test and to reach the First Certificate standard.

The first two exercises consist of five separate sentences, each with one missing word. The next four exercises are short passages, each with two missing words. The final four exercises are again short passages, but this time with three missing words.

In all the exercises, choose the word which best fits in the empty space. Answers and notes are on page 50.

Answers and notes are on page 50.

1   Peter would like to **(1)** ..... in Ireland.

   A dwell   **B** live   **C** occupy   **D** inhabit

2   Julie always **(2)** ..... the newspaper before breakfast.

   A read   **B** sent   **C** wrote   **D** made

3   Tony offered to look **(3)** ..... his nephew.

   A on   **B** after   **C** over   **D** into

4   Judith said that she did not know my cousin very **(4)** ..... .

   A badly   **B** lot   **C** properly   **D** well

5   The doctor said that George had broken a **(5)** ..... in his foot.

   A bone   **B** limb   **C** toe   **D** muscle

1   I've got an interview for a new **(1)** ..... on Friday.

   A employment   **B** work   **C** profession   **D** job

2   She **(2)** ..... lots of photos when she was on holiday.

   A took   **B** did   **C** made   **D** put

3   I want to buy her something **(3)** ..... nice for her birthday.

   A possibly   **B** actually   **C** really   **D** certainly

4   I know that you've already told me your name, but I'm afraid I've **(4)** ..... it.

   A remembered   **B** dropped   **C** forgotten   **D** known

5   They set off early **(5)** ..... the traffic was heavy.

   A as if   **B** in case   **C** if only   **D** even though

5

PRACTICE EXERCISE 3

It had always been John's ambition to **(1)** ..... a doctor but he finally realised that if he wanted to study medicine at university, he would have to begin working much **(2)** ..... at school than he had done so far.

1	**A** work	**B** qualify	**C** prepare	**D** be
2	**A** harder	**B** keener	**C** cleverer	**D** sooner

PRACTICE EXERCISE 4

The period of warm weather which the country has been enjoying for the **(1)** ..... few days is due to end tomorrow, when rain and storms are forecast for all parts of the country **(2)** ..... the north-west.

1	**A** recent	**B** past	**C** late	**D** former
2	**A** except	**B** less	**C** without	**D** apart

PRACTICE EXERCISE 5

Parents of pupils at Lowton High School are **(1)** ..... classes at the school in the evening **(2)** ..... to help them understand the ways in which certain subjects are now taught in school.

1	**A** attending	**B** making	**C** helping	**D** going
2	**A** so	**B** in addition	**C** for	**D** in order

PRACTICE EXERCISE 6

There will be no trains running on Wednesday **(1)** ..... a strike of railway workers throughout the country. It is expected that a normal **(2)** ..... will be operating by seven o'clock on Thursday morning.

1	**A** as a result	**B** according to	**C** because of	**D** by means
2	**A** service	**B** railway	**C** scale	**D** train

PRACTICE EXERCISE 7

One of the oldest shops in town will close at the **(1)** ..... of next week. Layton's butcher's shop has been **(2)** ..... customers with high quality meat for over ninety years but can no longer compete with the low prices on **(3)** ..... in the large supermarkets.

1	**A** completion	**B** finish	**C** end	**D** conclusion
2	**A** serving	**B** giving	**C** obtaining	**D** selling
3	**A** available	**B** bargain	**C** offer	**D** sale

PRACTICE EXERCISE 8

My cousin has now returned home to New Zealand after **(1)** ..... three weeks with us. I think that he really **(2)** ..... himself as he has written to me saying that he is already planning his next visit to England. He says, though, that it will take him at least two years to **(3)** ..... enough money for the air fare.

1	**A** remaining	**B** doing	**C** resting	**D** spending
2	**A** enjoyed	**B** loved	**C** pleased	**D** delighted
3	**A** collect	**B** save	**C** keep	**D** store

PRACTICE EXERCISE 9

Pupils at the local secondary school are **(1)** ..... really pleased this week as they have been told that they will have an extra week's summer holiday. The **(2)** ..... for the extra holiday is that work on repairing **(3)** ..... to the school following a fire at the beginning of August has not yet been completed.

1	**A** feeling	**B** seeming	**C** becoming	**D** being
2	**A** explanation	**B** purpose	**C** reason	**D** excuse
3	**A** injuries	**B** destruction	**C** damage	**D** ruin

PRACTICE EXERCISE 10

Peter and Sally Smith have been married for ten years and in that **(1)** ..... have never owned a television set as they always said that watching television was a **(2)** ..... of valuable time. Two months ago, they decided to buy a set and, ever **(3)** ..... then, have hardly left the house in the evening as they have been so busy watching television.

1	**A** interval	**B** term	**C** duration	**D** time
2	**A** lack	**B** waste	**C** loss	**D** need
3	**A** after	**B** following	**C** since	**D** later

DOING THE EXAM

1 Read through the passage to get an idea of what it is about. Do not try to fill in any of the empty spaces yet. Do *not* read through the list of suggested words.

2 Read the passage as far as the example **(0)** and look at the choice of words and the answer which is given.

3 Read the passage as far as the first empty space **(1)** which you have to fill in and then look at the choice of possible answers for the space. Read the words around the empty space and try to decide which is the most suitable answer. You will probably decide fairly quickly that one or two of the words are unsuitable but you may have to read the other words several times before you decide which is the correct answer.

4 When you have decided which is the correct answer, make a mark in pencil on the answer sheet by the letter which indicates the correct answer. If you cannot decide which is the correct answer, leave this item and move on to the next empty space.

5 Do the same for all 15 empty spaces.

6 When you have decided on the correct word for the final space **(15)**, go back to any of the items which you have not filled in. Think about the choice of words again and try to decide which word is most suitable. If, in the end, you really have no idea of the answer, mark any **one** of the four letters on the answer sheet.

7 When you are working through this part of the test, there may be times when you are fairly sure of the correct answer but feel that you would like to look at the item again later. If this happens, mark the letter which you think is correct on the answer sheet and put an asterisk (*) or some other kind of mark by the choice of words on the question paper to remind you to look at the item later. *Do not put this asterisk on the answer sheet.*

8 If you do return to one of the items mentioned in number 7 above and you decide to change the answer, rub out the answer you first thought of and then put your mark by the answer which you now think is correct.

Remember
- Only one of the four words will be correct. *Never* mark more than one letter for an answer.
- If you miss out an answer, make sure that when you put in the next answer, you put it by the correct number (that is to say that if, for example, you missed out answer 7, do not put answer 8 at the side of number 7).
- If you change your mind about an answer, remember to rub out the answer you had already indicated.
- Do not choose an answer because the letter by that word has not been used as a correct answer in the test so far.
- Always mark *one* of the letters on the answer sheet even if, after thinking about the item, you are simply guessing the answer. There is always a chance that you may be right.

EXAM EXERCISES

The four Exam Exercises which follow are not in order of difficulty. All of them are at First Certificate level.

EXAM EXERCISE 1

Choose which answer **A**, **B**, **C** or **D** best fits each space.

Example:

0   **A** set   **B** leave   **C** practise   **D** go

0	A	B	C	D
	▭	▭	▭	▬

NO LONGER A SECRET

As a young man, I would often **(0)** ..... walking in the country with friends at weekends. On one **(1)** ..... whilst out walking, we saw **(2)** ..... on a farm gate saying *Afternoon Teas*. We went into the farmhouse and were **(3)** ..... a huge plate of sandwiches and cake **(4)** ..... a pot of tea. No sooner had we finished than the farmer's wife, Mrs Gee, **(5)** ..... in with more sandwiches, cake and tea. When we left, we were amazed that the **(6)** ..... was so small; Mrs Gee was amazed that we did not **(7)** ..... any more to eat.

Whenever we went walking in that **(8)** ..... of the country, we always **(9)** ..... at Mrs Gee's and were always treated to a huge tea. One weekend, a friend who worked for a local newspaper came with us and was so **(10)** ..... with the food that he wrote an article about it in his paper.

It was more than a year before I **(11)** ..... Mrs Gee's farmhouse again and it was to my intense **(12)** ..... that I saw a sign saying *No Afternoon Teas*. Some time later, I learnt that it was because of the newspaper article that Mrs Gee had **(13)** ..... serving teas; following the **(14)** ..... of the article, she had had so many visitors that she simply could not manage.

Perhaps it is a good idea not to **(15)** ..... too many people know about one's discoveries.

1	**A** occasion	**B** time	**C** opportunity	**D** incident
2	**A** an announcement	**B** a notice	**C** an indication	**D** a signal
3	**A** presented	**B** taken	**C** provided	**D** served
4	**A** along with	**B** over and	**C** as well	**D** in addition
5	**A** carried	**B** got	**C** came	**D** brought
6	**A** account	**B** note	**C** invoice	**D** bill
7	**A** wish	**B** seek	**C** want	**D** ask
8	**A** piece	**B** part	**C** section	**D** quarter
9	**A** passed	**B** called	**C** stayed	**D** visited
10	**A** influenced	**B** excited	**C** impressed	**D** moved
11	**A** met	**B** arrived	**C** went	**D** approached
12	**A** shock	**B** anxiety	**C** disappointment	**D** concern
13	**A** stopped	**B** completed	**C** halted	**D** closed
14	**A** appearance	**B** advertisement	**C** aspect	**D** arrival
15	**A** make	**B** let	**C** invite	**D** allow

Answers and notes on page 51.

Choose which answer **A**, **B**, **C** or **D** best fits each space.

Example:

0   **A** feeling   **B** opinion   **C** sight   **D** belief

SAMUEL IRELAND

Samuel Ireland was an eighteenth century Englishman who had a poor **(0)** ..... of his son, William. **(1)** ..... what his father thought of him, William **(2)** ..... to prove himself.

As Samuel **(3)** ..... rare books and papers, William thought that the best **(4)** ..... to impress his father would be to **(5)** ..... something really rare for him. As Samuel was particularly **(6)** ..... in Shakespeare, the boy wrote a letter and told his father that it had been **(7)** ..... from Queen Elizabeth I to Shakespeare. His father was completely fooled by the letter.

William then produced many more Shakespearean items and told his father that they had been in a box **(8)** ..... to a rich man for whom he had done some **(9)** ..... . The old man had given William **(10)** ..... to take anything he wanted from the box. His father believed every word.

William even went so far as to write a play which he said was by Shakespeare. He called the play *Vortigern and Rowena* and he actually **(11)** ..... to have it performed in London. It was a total **(12)** ..... and William eventually **(13)** ..... having written it himself. In spite of this, his father, who had now changed his **(14)** ..... about William, refused to believe him and **(15)** ..... certain that everything he had found had been absolutely genuine.

1	**A** Aware	**B** Finding	**C** Knowing	**D** Conscious
2	**A** decided	**B** went	**C** came	**D** made
3	**A** picked	**B** obtained	**C** collected	**D** gathered
4	**A** manner	**B** way	**C** style	**D** plan
5	**A** give	**B** look	**C** search	**D** find
6	**A** fascinated	**B** keen	**C** eager	**D** interested
7	**A** sent	**B** transferred	**C** presented	**D** intended
8	**A** kept	**B** possessing	**C** owned	**D** belonging
9	**A** turns	**B** labour	**C** work	**D** tasks
10	**A** allowance	**B** right	**C** permission	**D** freedom
11	**A** managed	**B** achieved	**C** succeeded	**D** realised
12	**A** loss	**B** failure	**C** ruin	**D** defeat
13	**A** said	**B** granted	**C** stated	**D** admitted
14	**A** mind	**B** idea	**C** thought	**D** decision
15	**A** left	**B** remained	**C** stopped	**D** rested

Answers and notes on page 51.

Choose which answer **A**, **B**, **C** of **D** best fits each space.

Example:

0   **A** regarded   **B** called   **C** counted   **D** thought

0	A	B	C	D

SMOKING

For much of the twentieth century smoking was **(0)** ..... of as a fashionable activity. However, as the century progressed, an increasing **(1)** ..... of scientific research showed that tobacco could have a very **(2)** ..... effect on health.

Throughout the world, governments have tried different methods to persuade people to **(3)** ..... smoking and there can now be few people who are not aware of the **(4)** ..... between smoking and serious illness. In spite of this, many people **(5)** ..... to smoke. Smokers find that a cigarette or a pipe **(6)** ..... them relax and it seems right that they should have the **(7)** ..... to smoke if it gives them some pleasure and relief from stress.

It can be **(8)** ..... that smoking is not so bad for **(9)** ..... as drinking alcohol; people who drink too much alcohol become drunk and can be a very real danger to others, **(10)** ..... if they are driving a car; at least smokers are a danger only to themselves. However, organisations which **(11)** ..... people to stop smoking claim that if a person smokes in a place where other people are **(12)** ..... , the health of these other people is put at **(13)** ..... because they also will be **(14)** ..... in smoke from cigarettes. If this is really the **(15)** ..... , it may be that smoking should always be forbidden in all public places.

1	A	amount	B	number	C	total	D	sum
2	A	wicked	B	unlucky	C	harmful	D	wrong
3	A	stop over	B	get away	C	give up	D	drop off
4	A	link	B	combination	C	union	D	joint
5	A	remain	B	continue	C	keep	D	carry
6	A	allows	B	aids	C	permits	D	helps
7	A	independence	B	ability	C	freedom	D	occasion
8	A	discussed	B	argued	C	known	D	told
9	A	public	B	country	C	society	D	community
10	A	especially	B	mainly	C	principally	D	generally
11	A	make	B	encourage	C	manage	D	achieve
12	A	attending	B	situated	C	placed	D	present
13	A	risk	B	fate	C	chance	D	threat
14	A	getting	B	putting	C	sending	D	breathing
15	A	thing	B	case	C	product	D	condition

Answers and notes on page 52.

Choose which answer **A**, **B**, **C** or **D** best fits each space.

Example:

0 **A** intend   **B** experience   **C** think   **D** regard

NOT SAYING WHAT WE MEAN

Most people **(0)** ..... that when they speak, they say what they mean. In fact this is not always **(1)** ..... . Sometimes some people find it more effective to get their message **(2)** ..... by actually saying the opposite of what they mean.

A young woman gave an **(3)** ..... of this when she **(4)** ..... that, as a girl, she always had to ask her father's **(5)** ..... if she wanted to go out. He never said no but she could **(6)** ..... from the way he said yes whether or not he wanted her to go. If he said something like "Yes, if you want, you can go," she knew that he was not **(7)** ..... on the idea. It was not only the words but also his **(8)** ..... of voice and the expression on his face that told her how he **(9)** ..... .

Some people might wonder why the father did not **(10)** ..... say no if he did not want his daughter to go out. He might have thought that he really was giving her a **(11)** ..... . Indeed, the daughter herself might have felt that she was making up her own **(12)** ..... as her father never actually refused her **(13)** ..... . In the final analysis, the father's way of refusing **(14)** ..... arguments and probably led to a better **(15)** ..... between the two of them.

1	**A** thus	**B** at	**C** that	**D** so
2	**A** on	**B** across	**C** off	**D** along
3	**A** indication	**B** occasion	**C** incident	**D** example
4	**A** showed	**B** explained	**C** suggested	**D** demonstrated
5	**A** allowance	**B** support	**C** permission	**D** authority
6	**A** tell	**B** inform	**C** find	**D** notice
7	**A** keen	**B** eager	**C** anxious	**D** enthusiastic
8	**A** level	**B** manner	**C** style	**D** tone
9	**A** appeared	**B** felt	**C** thought	**D** was
10	**A** simply	**B** purely	**C** only	**D** merely
11	**A** preference	**B** selection	**C** possibility	**D** choice
12	**A** decision	**B** wish	**C** mind	**D** idea
13	**A** inquiries	**B** requests	**C** questions	**D** favours
14	**A** escaped	**B** ceased	**C** prevented	**D** checked
15	**A** relationship	**B** association	**C** communication	**D** knowledge

Answers and notes on page 52.

LOOKING AT PART 2

In this part of the Use of English paper you have a passage to read in which there are sixteen empty spaces where words are missing. You must decide what the missing words must be. The difference between this test and the test in Part 1 is that you do not have a set of words to choose from – you must think of the missing word yourself.

It is important to note that, as in the first part of this paper, the first empty space is an example and always has the number **0**. The correct word to fill this space is written above the title of the passage. Be careful not to put the answer for **0** as your first answer – remember this is an example which has been done for you. The questions in Part 2 are numbered 16–30.

THE MISSING WORDS

The missing words here will often be a little different from the missing words in Part 1 of the paper. In Part 1 you have to select words for their meaning; in Part 2 you are thinking of words which fit best with the way the passage is written. If this difference seems complicated, do not worry about it; all that you have to do is to think of the most suitable words to fill the empty spaces.

In this part of the paper the missing words are likely to be prepositions*, pronouns*, auxiliary verbs*, articles* and words that link two parts of a sentence. You will not often find that the missing words are nouns*.

FILLING IN THE ANSWER SHEET

In this part of the paper you simply have to write the answer in the appropriate place on the answer sheet. You must spell the word correctly. It is usually better to 'print' your answer rather than to use your normal handwriting. This means that if you think the missing word is *which*, it is better for you to write the word in capital letters:

WHICH

rather than in joined-up letters:

which

The reason for this is that if your writing is not clear and there is doubt about your spelling of the word, you will not be given a mark.

The empty space must be filled by only *one* word. If you think that two or more words are suitable, you will have to choose and write only *one*. If you write more than one word on the answer sheet for any item, you will not be given a mark for that answer.

Make sure you do not write in the last column of the answer sheet, marked *Do not write here.*

WORDS WHICH ARE TESTED

Although there are fewer words which may be tested in this part of the paper than in Part 1, there are still many different words which may appear. It is almost certain that some of the missing words will be prepositions* (often as part of a phrasal verb*). Quite often the missing words will be very short (e.g. *a, and, or*).

Below is a list of some words and types of words that are likely to appear. All of the sentences in the first two Practice Exercises contain examples of these types of words. (Please note, this list is by no means a complete list of words that may appear in the test.)

Articles*
  a, an, the

Pronouns*
  I,   he,   she,   we,   they
  me,   you,   him,   her,   it,   us,   them
  myself,   yourself,   himself,   herself,   ourselves,   itself,   themselves
  my,   your,   his,   her,   our,   its,   their

Negative words*
  not,   no,   nobody,   nothing,   nowhere

Indefinite words*
  anybody,   anything,   anywhere,   any
  somebody,   something,   somewhere,   somehow,   some

Auxiliary verbs*
  am,   is,   are,   was,   were
  being,   been
  have,   has,   had
  do,   did
  will,   would,   should
  can,   could,   may,   might,   must,   ought

Linking words*
  and,   but,   or
  if,   how,   why,   where,   when,   while,   as,   after,   since,   because,   although
  who,   which,   that,   whose

Prepositions*
  in,   at,   by,   from,   to,   with,   on,   off,   etc.

General
  there (as in *there is*, *there are*, etc.)
  this,   that,   these,   those
  even though,   even if
  enough to: Claire is not old *enough to* drive.
  few: A *few* people were there.
                  A *few of* the people spoke to me.
  too ..... to: He was *too* tired *to* show any interest in what was happening.
  so ..... that: The traffic moved *so* quickly *that* we arrived early.
                  We drove quickly *so that* we would arrive early.
  so ..... as: We drove quickly *so as* to arrive early.
  Comparatives*: Anne is *more* generous *than* Sally.
                  Anne is *less* generous *than* Sally.
                  Anne is *as* generous *as* Sally.

PRACTICE EXERCISES

On the next page are ten Practice Exercises for you to work through before beginning the full Exam Exercises. These Practice Exercises are far shorter than the Exam Exercises and also rather easier. They will help you to get used to doing this sort of test and to reach the First Certificate standard. The first two exercises consist of ten separate sentences each with one missing word, the next four exercises are short passages each with two missing words, the next three exercises are again short passages, but this time with three missing words, and the last exercise is a slightly longer passage with eight missing words.

In all the exercises, write down the word which best fits in the empty space. Answers and notes are on pages 52 and 53.

PRACTICE EXERCISE 1

1 Do you know where we **(1)** .... supposed to go now?
2 I think I've had **(2)** .... much to eat.
3 She gets on well with both her sister **(3)** .... her brother.
4 The children went to the dentist to have **(4)** .... teeth checked.
5 I could not find **(5)** .... to sit down.
6 Mary should **(6)** .... arrived back by now.
7 My neighbour told me **(7)** .... had happened.
8 That is the house **(8)** .... my grandfather was born.
9 Helen told me that she had still **(9)** .... finished decorating the house.
10 If you were going to the party, I **(10)** .... come with you.

PRACTICE EXERCISE 2

1 That was **(1)** .... only time he'd ever been to London.
2 Linda sings much better **(2)** .... her brother.
3 The teacher accused me of **(3)** .... rude.
4 It was **(4)** .... dark that we could not find our way out of the cellar.
5 The furniture **(5)** .... bought by a man wearing a grey suit.
6 Do you know anybody **(6)** .... lives in Manchester?
7 I helped him with his homework even **(7)** .... I was tired.
8 I will help him with his homework, even **(8)** .... I am tired.
9 I don't have **(9)** .... money to buy a car.
10 Did you see **(10)** .... strange happening?

PRACTICE EXERCISE 3

My sister decided to spend her holidays at the seaside but she **(1)** .... not really enjoy herself very much as she said that **(2)** .... poured with rain every day.

PRACTICE EXERCISE 4

My uncle Tom will be eighty-five next month and has decided that he is **(1)** .... old to keep on doing all the work in the garden himself. He has asked one of his neighbours to come in and help him for two **(2)** .... three days a week.

PRACTICE EXERCISE 5

The local library will be closed for **(1)** .... whole of next week as the building is to be completely redecorated. As many people are at present **(2)** .... holiday, it is hoped that this will not cause too much inconvenience.

PRACTICE EXERCISE 6

Walter and Doris Wayne are celebrating fifty years of married life **(1)** .... weekend. The two of them first met in the chocolate factory **(2)** .... they both worked for over forty years.

PRACTICE EXERCISE 7

Michael Richards had a most unfortunate experience last week. He **(1)** .... been to visit his brother who was in hospital with a broken leg, but he slipped on the steps as he **(2)** .... leaving the hospital and broke his ankle. Half an hour later, he found himself in a bed just a **(3)** .... metres away from his brother.

PRACTICE EXERCISE 8

Roy Taylor, a local businessman, has won over £100,000 in a competition organised by a national newspaper. Mr Taylor has said that he intends to give most of the money **(1)** .... as he does not really need it. However, he will keep **(2)** .... of it to buy a new car **(3)** .... his wife.

The local technical college is organising a course **(1)** .... aims to help people understand British life and customs. **(2)** .... the course is mainly aimed at people who were not born in this country, anybody is welcome to attend. The course **(3)** .... begin at 7.30 p.m. on Tuesday, 10th January and will run for ten weeks.

PRACTICE EXERCISE 9

I went with my parents to the airport yesterday to meet my sister, Jane, **(1)** .... was coming home after spending a year in Canada. The plane **(2)** .... not arrive at eight o'clock **(3)** .... it was due. We tried to find out when the plane would **(4)** .... arriving but **(5)** .... seemed to know **(6)** .... was happening. We **(7)** .... getting increasingly worried but then we saw the plane land and about half **(8)** .... hour later my sister appeared looking tired but happy.

PRACTICE EXERCISE 10

DOING THE EXAM

1 Read through the passage to get an idea of what it is about. Do not try to fill in any of the empty spaces yet.

2 Read the passage as far as the example **(0)** and look at the answer which is given.

3 Read the passage as far as the first empty space **(16)** which you have to fill in, and try to decide what the missing word is. It will often help to read to the end of the sentence, as there may be clues after the empty space.

4 When you have decided what the missing word is, write it on the answer sheet by the number for that space. If you cannot decide which is the correct answer, leave this item and move on to the next empty space.

5 Make sure that you spell the answer correctly and that your writing is clear.

6 Do the same for all 15 empty spaces.

7 When you have decided on the correct word for the final space **(30)**, go back to any of the items which you have not filled in. Try again to decide what the missing word is. If in the end you really have no idea of the answer, write any word on the answer sheet. There is always a chance that it might be right.

8 When you are working through this part of the test, there may be times when you are fairly sure of the correct answer but feel that you would like to look at the item again later. If this happens, write the word which you think is correct on the answer sheet and put an asterisk (*) or some other kind of mark by the empty space on the question paper. This will remind you to look at the item later. *Do not put this asterisk on the answer sheet.*

9 If you do return to one of the items mentioned in number 8 above and you decide to change the answer, rub out the answer you first thought of and then write in the answer which you now think is correct.

Remember

• Write only *one* word for each answer. If you write more than one word, you will not get a mark.

• If you miss out an answer, make sure that when you put in the next answer, you put it by the correct number (that is to say that if, for example, you missed out answer 17, do not put the answer for 18 at the side of number 17).

• If you change your mind about an answer, remember to rub out the answer you had already indicated.

• Always write in an answer, even if you have no idea what the correct answer is. It is better to make a guess rather than to leave an answer blank.

EXAM EXERCISES

The four Exam Exercises which follow are not in order of difficulty. All of them are at First Certificate level.

In each exercise, read the text and think of the word which best fits each space. Use only **one** word in each space. There is an example **(0)** at the beginning of each exercise.

EXAM EXERCISE 1   Example:

0 | than | 0

THE ISLE OF WIGHT

The Isle of Wight lies less **(0)** ..... five kilometres off the south coast of England. It is **(1)** ..... of the country's best-known islands but, in **(2)** ..... of the short distance **(3)** ..... the island and the rest of England, a bridge has never **(4)** ..... built to link the two. In order to get **(5)** ..... , you must take a boat, or a private plane.

The island, **(6)** ..... is about 37 kilometres in length and 22 kilometres wide, has a population of 120,000, although this rises in summer when tourists arrive **(7)** ..... large numbers. People come here **(8)** ..... the peace and quiet; it is **(9)** ..... area of great natural beauty with delightful open countryside and long clean beaches. Even the towns, although busy in summer, still have an atmosphere of tranquility and old-fashioned charm.

It was in the nineteenth century that people began to take holidays on the Isle of Wight. The **(10)** ..... famous visitor to the island at this time was, without doubt, Queen Victoria. The royal family **(11)** ..... bought Osborne House on the island in 1845 and the Queen, **(12)** ..... loved the house, spent much of her life here. After her death in 1901, the new King, Edward VII, gave Osborne House to the nation as he **(13)** ..... not share **(14)** ..... mother's love of the house and had **(15)** ..... wish to live in it.

EXAM EXERCISE 2   Example:

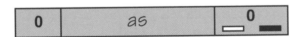

0 | as | 0

ROBERT BURNS

Robert Burns is generally regarded **(0)** ..... the national poet of Scotland. He wrote poems using the Scottish dialect even though it **(1)** ..... not considered fashionable to **(2)** ..... so.

He was born near the town of Alloway in 1759 and was **(3)** ..... eldest of seven children. His father was a poor farmer and, from the age of thirteen, Robert had to help working on the farm. The work was hard and, unfortunately, the farm made very **(4)** ..... money. Robert found some relief in drinking in local inns and in reading and writing poetry.

Robert grew increasingly tired of the hard work on the farm and, soon **(5)** ..... his father had died, he decided to make a new start **(6)** ..... going to live in Jamaica, but he was **(7)** ..... of money for the fare. Some friends thought that his poems might **(8)** ..... worth some money and suggested that he should have **(9)** ..... published. The first edition of his poems was published in 1786 and was **(10)** ..... instant success. Robert **(11)** ..... up his plans to leave and decided that he **(12)** ..... definitely stay in Scotland.

More **(13)** ..... his poems were published over the next few years but, unfortunately, now that he **(14)** ..... more money, Robert began drinking very heavily and in 1796 caught a fever from **(15)** ..... he died at the early age of 37.

Example:

| 0 | *to* | 0 |

A LONG-DISTANCE PIGEON

Pigeons are birds which are able **(0)** ..... find their way home even when they have been taken a great distance away. For this reason a sport **(1)** ..... as pigeon racing has developed. A **(2)** ..... days before a race, the pigeons are taken hundreds of kilometres away from **(3)** ..... homes and, on the day of the race, they are released to fly back home. The bird which arrives home **(4)** ..... the shortest length of time is the winner. Unfortunately, it is **(5)** ..... fact that birds sometimes get lost and **(6)** ..... never seen again.

This apparently **(7)** ..... to a pigeon belonging to a man from the south-west of England. The bird had **(8)** ..... taken to the south of France, **(9)** ..... the race began, and had set **(10)** ..... with the other birds, but had never arrived home. Two years later, the owner **(11)** ..... surprised to receive a letter saying that the bird was at the house of a pigeon owner in China. The man **(12)** ..... had found the bird had discovered the address of the English owner from the number on the ring round the pigeon's leg.

It is hard to believe that the pigeon could have flown **(13)** ..... the way from France to China – a distance of more **(14)** ..... 8,000 kilometres; the bird had probably landed **(15)** ..... a ship which was going to China.

Example:

| 0 | *are* | 0 |

RHYMING SLANG

If you go to London, you **(0)** ..... quite likely to meet a 'cockney'. According **(1)** ..... the traditional definition, a cockney is a person who **(2)** ..... born in the part of London **(3)** ..... the sound of the bells of the church of St Mary-le-Bow can **(4)** ..... heard. Generally, though, the term is used to indicate any working-class person **(5)** ..... lives in the east end of London.

Some cockneys have a way of speaking which is **(6)** ..... as *rhyming slang*. In rhyming slang, **(7)** ..... of using the normal word for something, cockneys use a word which is different but which has **(8)** ..... similar sound to the word intended. There are hundreds of words in rhyming slang but **(9)** ..... of the best known examples is the phrase *apples and pears*, **(10)** ..... means *stairs* because *stairs* has the same sound as *pears*. Another example is *Hampstead Heath*, meaning *teeth*.

If this seems all very confusing, **(11)** ..... not worry as nowadays many cockneys are **(12)** ..... to use rhyming slang well, and **(13)** ..... those who can do **(14)** ..... would not normally use it when speaking to a person from another part **(15)** ..... Britain, and certainly not when speaking to someone from a different country.

Answers and notes on pages 54 – 55.

LOOKING AT PART 3

There are ten items in this part of the Use of English paper. Each item consists of three lines; on the first line there is a complete sentence, on the second line there is just one word, the *key word*, and on the third line is a sentence from which some words are missing. You have to think of the words which you would have to put into the second sentence along with the key word to make it mean more or less the same as the first sentence.

You must use *not more than five words* to complete this second sentence. One of the words which you *must* use is the key word, that is the word given between the two sentences. This word must *not be changed* in any way. The questions in Part 3 are numbered 31– 40.

In this part of the paper every item is worth 2 marks.

FILLING IN THE ANSWER SHEET

On your answer sheet for this part of the paper, there are empty spaces where you must write your answers.

Do *not* write out the whole of the second sentence, write out only the words that you wish to put in the sentence. Remember that you must not write more than five words including the key word, although you may write fewer than five (the answer may consist of two, three, four or five words).

You must *not* change the key word in any way. This means that if the key word is *say*, you cannot change this to *says*, *saying*, *said*, or anything else. The word must remain as *say*.

As in Part 2, it is usually better to print your answer in capital letters rather than to use joined-up handwriting, so that your spelling of the words is clear.

Make sure you do not write in the last column of the answer sheet, marked *Do not write here*.

DECIDING ON THE MISSING WORDS

There is a vast number of expressions which can be tested in this part of the paper and it is quite impossible to make a list of all of them. However, some types of expressions are likely to appear fairly often; there are examples of some of them below.

Look at these pairs of sentences and note what changes have to be made.

Reporting speech
When reporting what somebody has said, the verb* moves back to an earlier tense* (this means present becomes past, *will* becomes *would*, etc.). In addition *I* becomes *he/she*, *we* becomes *us*, etc.

He said, 'I am ready'.	He said that he was ready.
She said, 'I will phone later'.	She said that she would phone later.
They said, 'We saw him there'.	They said that they had seen him there.

When reporting a question which does not begin with a question word such as *Who*, *Where*, *Why*, *How*, *When*, *What*, you must make the question into an ordinary statement and put *if* at the beginning of it. (Do not put a question mark at the end of the sentence when you are reporting a question).

He said, 'Does Mary live in Bristol?'	He asked if Mary lived in Bristol.
She asked, 'Have you been to Scotland?'	She asked if I had been to Scotland.

Expressions to do with past time
It is 3 years since I saw him.

I last saw her in 1995.

I had never been to Paris before.

I have not seen him for 3 years.

I have not seen her since 1995.

It was the first time I had been to Paris.

Active to Passive*
The police caught the thief.

The thief was caught by the police.

Comparatives*
Jane is taller than Paul.

The play was more exciting than the film.

Paul is not as tall as Jane.

The film was not as exciting as the play.

or

The film was less exciting than the play

Superlatives*
She is the cleverest person I know.

I do not know anyone cleverer than her.

or

I do not know anyone as clever as her.

Belong
Mary asked, 'Whose is this watch?'

Mary wanted to know who the watch belonged to.

Despite/in spite of
I like him despite his silliness.

We went out in spite of the rain.

I like him even though he is silly.

We went out even though it was raining.

How
I had forgotten he was so tall.

I had forgotten how tall he was.

If/unless
He did not win because he was lazy.

I'll go only if you come with me.

I think you should leave.

He didn't phone, so I couldn't go.

If he had not been lazy, he would have won.

I won't go unless you come with me.

If I were you, I would leave.

If he had phoned, I could have gone.

In case
I'm taking some sandwiches as I might get hungry.

I'm taking some sandwiches in case I get hungry.

Necessary
He did not need to buy a ticket.

It was not necessary for him to buy a ticket.

Only/except/apart from
Only John knows the truth.

Nobody knows the truth except John.

or

Nobody apart from John knows the truth.

Remember/forget + anything, anybody, etc.
I do not remember anything he said.

I have forgotten everything he said.

Responsible
Tom has to check all the rooms.

Tom is responsible for checking all the rooms.

Run out of
I have run out of money.

I have no money left.

So
The party was so boring that we left early.

The book was so dear that I could not buy it.

It was such a boring party that we left early.

The book was too dear for me to buy.

Sorry

She is sorry she annoyed you.	She regrets annoying/having annoyed you.
He said he was sorry he had been angry.	He apologised for being/having been angry.
I was sorry to have left so early.	I wish I had not left so early.

Take

They walked to Leeds in three hours.   It took them three hours to walk to Leeds.

Usually

It is not like Bill to be selfish.   Bill is not usually selfish.

Want/rather/prefer

He does not want to sing.

He would rather not sing.
or
He would prefer not to sing.

Without

He did not ring the bell before he came in.   He came in without ringing the bell.

DOING THE EXAM

1 Read the two sentences and the key word.

2 Try to think of words along with the key word to fill the space in the second sentence.

3 Count the number of words you have thought of and, if there are more than five, think of another way of filling the space.

4 Write your answer in the space provided. If you miss out a question, make sure that you write your answer to the next question in the correct space.

Remember

• Do *not* write more than five words.

• Do *not* change the key word in any way.

• Make sure the meaning of the second sentence is similar to that of the first sentence.

• Make sure that your spelling is correct.

EXAM EXERCISES

There are no separate Practice Exercises in this part of the book. However, there are six Exam Exercises. The first two are based directly on the examples above. Answers and notes are on pages 56 and 57.

EXAM EXERCISE 1

Complete the second sentence so that it has a similar meaning to the first sentence, using the word given. **Do not change the word given**. You must use between two and five words including the word given.

1 Last week was the first time she had ever watched television.
   never

   She .... last week.

2 Several tourists saw the accident.
   several

   The accident .... tourists.

3 'Do you like travelling by train?' asked Kate.
   I

   Kate asked me .... travelling by train.

4 That is the biggest dog I have ever seen.
   dog

   I have .... than that one.

5 I am surprised that Mary is so happy after all the problems she has had.
   happy

   I am surprised at .... after all the problems she has had.

6 I feel that I cannot trust anyone apart from my sister.
   person

   I feel that my sister is .... trust.

7 I think you should buy the car.
   you

   If .... buy the car.

8 He did not put a stamp on the letter he posted.
   stamp

   He posted the letter .... it.

9 She will have to send in an application form.
   necessary

   It .... to send in an application form.

10 The man was so unpleasant that I began to lose my temper with him.
   man

   He was .... that I began to lose my temper with him.

Answers and notes on page 56.

Complete the second sentence so that it has a similar meaning to the first sentence, using the word given. **Do not change the word given**. You must use between two and five words including the word given.

EXAM EXERCISE 2

1 I said I was sorry that I had broken the glass.
   for

   I .... the glass.

2 He does not spend much money because he is afraid of losing his job.
   case

   He does not spend much money .... his job.

3 Tom can sing better than Jane.
   as

   Jane .... Tom.

4 They found the answer in ten minutes.
   to

   It .... find the answer.

5 We got to sleep even though it was noisy last night.
   spite

   We got to sleep .... last night.

6 They would not go out unless it stopped raining.
   only

   They .... it stopped raining.

7 He had forgotten everything about his time in the army.
   not

   He .... about his time in the army.

8 I do not want to ride in his car.
   rather

   I .... ride in his car.

9 "Where did we buy the television?" Lucy asked her husband.
   where

   Lucy asked if her husband knew .... the television.

10 The people at work were friendlier than our neighbours.
   than

   Our neighbours were .... the people at work.

Answers and notes on page 56.

EXAM EXERCISE 3

Complete the second sentence so that it has a similar meaning to the first sentence, using the word given. **Do not change the word given**. You must use between two and five words including the word given.

1 He went on holiday yesterday.
   yesterday

   It .... went on holiday.

2 I cannot speak German very well.
   speaking

   I am not .... German.

3 Few people turned up for the show.
   many

   There .... the show.

4 Sarah had not expected her interview to be so short.
   was

   Sarah's interview .... expected.

5 We did not go for a picnic because it was raining heavily this morning.
   of

   We did not go for a picnic because .... this morning.

6 It took Raymond only two months to learn to drive.
   drive

   Raymond .... only two months.

7 An old dog followed my father home.
   followed

   My father .... an old dog.

8 Kate is taller than me.
   as

   I .... Kate.

9 Nobody agreed with me apart from Bill.
   person

   Bill .... agreed with me.

10 I was sorry not to meet your friend.
   I

   I wish .... your friend.

Answers and notes on page 56.

Complete the second sentence so that it has a similar meaning to the first sentence, using the word given. **Do not change the word given**. You must use between two and five words including the word given.

EXAM EXERCISE 4

1 It is three years since I last saw Paul.
   not

   I .... three years.

2 Could she possibly ring me again tomorrow?
   possible

   Would .... to ring me again tomorrow?

3 I would prefer it if nobody heard about what happened this morning.
   want

   I don't .... about what happened this morning.

4 John has not written so I cannot tell you the arrangements.
   have

   If John .... told you the arrangements.

5 I was unable to lift the box because it was so heavy.
   me

   The box was .... lift.

6 Tony apologised for not answering my letter.
   that

   Tony said he was .... answered my letter.

7 My boss phoned the office every day despite being on holiday.
   he

   My boss phoned the office every day even .... on holiday.

8 I saw nobody that I knew at the market this morning.
  not

  I .... that I knew at the market this morning.

9 He took a long time to decide what he wanted to study at college.
  come

  He took a long time .... about what he wanted to study at college.

10 "I'll be home late this evening," Mr Jones said to his wife.
  be

  Mr Jones told his wife .... late that evening.

Answers and notes on page 57.

EXAM EXERCISE 5

Complete the second sentence so that it has a similar meaning to the first sentence, using the word given. **Do not change the word given.** You must use between two and five words including the word given.

1 You should take an overcoat because it might get cold later.
  case

  You should take an overcoat .... later.

2 They intend working abroad when they finish college.
  intention

  It is .... abroad when they finish college.

3 "I saw your boss on the train this morning," Mr Jay said to his wife.
  seen

  Mr Jay told his wife that he .... on the train that morning.

4 Only club members may vote in the election.
  not

  People .... club members may not vote in the election.

5 Everybody in the town knew my uncle.
  known

  My uncle .... everybody in the town.

6 The teacher wanted to know who had broken the window.
  responsible

  The teacher wanted to know .... the window.

7 I think you should phone John this evening.
  you

  If I .... phone John this evening.

8 I will lend you some money only if you promise to pay me back tomorrow.
  lend

  I won't .... you promise to pay me back tomorrow.

9 She has never left the house since her son was born.
the

She has never left the house since .... her son.

10 I ate too much at the party last night.
much

I should not .... at the party last night.

Answers and notes on page 57.

Complete the second sentence so that it has a similar meaning to the first sentence, using the word given. **Do not change the word given**. You must use between two and five words including the word given.

1 My brother is not happy in spite of having lots of money.
even

My brother is not happy .... lots of money.

2 I asked my sister to take me to the airport.
she

I asked my sister .... me to the airport.

3 We have not been to the theatre for several months now.
last

It is several months .... to the theatre.

4 You need a special key to open that door.
you

You can open that door only .... a special key.

5 He had run out of money by the third day of his holiday.
money

He did not .... by the third day of his holiday.

6 "We have just bought a new car," said Mr and Mrs Brown.
just

Mr and Mrs Brown said that .... a new car.

7 I did not have enough time last night to phone you.
short

I did not phone you because .... last night.

8 Carol had never ridden a horse before.
the

It .... Carol had ridden a horse.

9 Philip apologised for his bad behaviour last night.
had

Philip said he was sorry that .... last night.

10 Please, don't leave the windows open.
mind

Would you .... the windows open.

Answers and notes on page 57.

25

LOOKING AT THE EXAM

In this part of the Use of English paper you have to read a passage and find mistakes. The passage will be the type of writing which you may do yourself, so it may seem like part of a letter.

The passage will contain 17 (or occasionally 18) lines. Some of these lines have a mistake in them but others are perfectly correct.

All the lines have a number. The first line has the number 0 and the second line has the number 00. These two lines are for examples; one will be an example of a line which has a mistake in it and the other will be an example of a line which is perfectly correct. The answers for the examples will be given above the passage (see the Exam Exercises).

Sometimes you will find an extra line at the bottom of the passage which does not have a number. This line is there simply because it has not been possible to write the whole of the passage in the 17 lines. This line is not part of the test and you must not look for mistakes here. The questions in Part 4 are numbered 41–55.

MISTAKES AND CORRECT LINES

The mistakes are always extra words which should not be present in a sentence. The mistakes are *never* spelling errors.

The mistakes will often be short words such as prepositions*, pronouns* or articles*. However, this will not always be so, and sometimes the extra word will be considerably longer. At times the extra word will be one which wrongly changes the tense* of the passage.

HOW TO DO THE EXAM

Here is an example of a line which has an error in it:
  My brother said that he would do like to work in a bank.
The mistake is *do* because it does not make sense in this line. If this line appeared in a passage in the exam, you would write *do* on the answer sheet.

Now, here is an example of a line which is perfectly correct:
  My brother said that he would like to work in a bank.
There is no mistake in this line, so you would put a tick (✓) on the answer sheet.

Sometimes you will find a word in a line which is not absolutely necessary to the meaning of a sentence. Such a word is not an error. Here is a sentence which contains an extra word:
  My brother said that he would really like to work in a bank.
The sentence is perfectly correct without the word *really* but *really* is certainly not a mistake – it gives us some extra information, telling us that my brother's wish to work in a bank is strong. The word is not absolutely necessary but it is certainly not a mistake.

Below are six sentences, all of which contain at least one word which is not absolutely necessary for the sentence to make sense. In three of the sentences the extra word makes the sentence wrong, in three the word simply gives us some extra information. Try to work out which are the correct sentences and which are the ones containing an error.

1 Peter is saving up so that he can buy all a new car.
2 My friend had to work in London all last week.

3 I was much happier when I lived in Scotland.
4 I will not be as much busy tomorrow as I am today.
5 I see John every daily.
6 I have seen every film that she made.

Sentences 2, 3 and 6 are correct sentences even though they all contain a word (*all, much, that*) which is not vital to the meaning of the sentence. Sentences 1, 4 and 5 all contain extra words (*all, much, every*) which are wrong.

FILLING IN THE ANSWER SHEET

In this part of the paper you have to write the extra word on the answer sheet for lines where you find an incorrect word, or a tick (✓) for lines with no extra incorrect word. Make sure you do not write in the last column of the answer sheet marked **Do not write here**.

SOME EXTRA WORDS TO LOOK FOR

There are many reasons why words might be wrong – they may have the wrong meaning, they may be wrongly placed in a set phrase, they may make the grammar of the sentence incorrect. Below are some examples of the type of errors to look for.

Verb tenses*
The words *have* and *had* are likely to appear quite often in most passages. These can sometimes be the extra word when they lead to an incorrect change in the main narrative* tense* of the passage, as shown in the two sentences below.

1 We caught the bus into town and I *have* bought the tickets at the cinema.
2 He went into the bathroom and *had* washed his hands.

Sometimes *had* will be in an impossible combination, e.g. *must had, should had, could had, might had*. In these cases, it is usually *must, should, could, might* which is the wrong word. Be careful also with *being* and *been*. In the two following examples both sentences are correct only if *being* and *been* are taken out.

1 The singer is *being* famous all over the world.
2 He has *been* finished all his work.

Double negatives*
It is wrong in English to have a double negative. This means that if you have a word such as *not* or *never*, you may not follow it with another negative word (e.g. *nobody, nowhere, nothing, no*).

1 I *never* saw *nothing* happening near the house.

Here the extra word is *never* as the sentence makes sense if you miss it out. If *nothing* is missed out, the sentence does not make sense.

Position
Quite often a word is wrong because it is in the wrong position and the sentence makes perfect sense without it. If the word had been in another position, it would have been correct. Look at the examples which follow.

1 I left after shortly ten o'clock.   (*shortly* should follow *left*: *I left shortly after ten o'clock.*)
2 We went all to the theatre.   (*all* should be after *we*: *We all went to the theatre.*)
3 It heavily rained that morning.   (*heavily* should be after *rained*: *It rained heavily that morning.*)
4 She has not been yet to see me.   (*yet* should be after *not* or after *me*: *She has not yet been to see me* or *She has not been to see me yet.*)

Comparisons

Remember that if you have the comparative* of an adjective* ending in *-er*, or the superlative* ending in *-est*, you must not put *more* or *most* with these words. *More* and *most* in the following sentences would be wrong:

1 The lesson was *more* easier this week.
2 That is the *most* tallest building in the world.

Remember that *better* and *worse* are comparatives and that *best* and *worst* are superlatives. They must, therefore, *not* be used with *more* or *most*.

(Note: The adjective *clever*, even though it ends in *-er*, is not a comparative and so you may write either *cleverer* or *more clever*.)

When *more* is used before a number, the word *than* must be placed between *more* and the number. Look at these two examples:

1   There were *more than* 200 people at the concert.
2   There were *more* 200 people at the concert.

The first sentence is perfectly correct. The second sentence is wrong. If we take *more* out of the second sentence, it makes sense (although it does not mean the same as the first sentence). The same rule applies to *less*.

Prepositions*

Prepositions are quite often the extra word. Below are just three examples.
· The preposition *of* is not normally used after *enough, too much, too many, so much, so many, too little, so little*.
· The preposition *to* is not used immediately in front of the word *home*.
· Be careful with verbs* such as *give, lend, send, offer*. Note the following sentences:

1 She gave John a present.
2 She gave a present to John.

When the person is mentioned immediately after *give, lend, send, offer*, etc., *to* is not used, but when the thing that the person is giving (lending, sending, offering, etc.) is mentioned immediately after the verb, then *to* must be used in front of the person, as in the examples above.

Articles*

Be careful with articles (*the, a, an*) as you will often find they should not be present.

When + will

After *when* in a statement, you do not use *will* or *shall* when referring to future time.

1 I will tell you when I see you.
2 He will come when he is ready.

(You do use a future tense if *When* is the beginning of a question, e.g. *When will I see you?*)

Phrasal Verbs*

Be careful about phrasal verbs. You will sometimes find in Part 4 of this paper that a verb is followed by a preposition. This may or may not be a correct use of a phrasal verb. Check carefully.

PRACTICE EXERCISES

Opposite are five Practice Exercises, each consisting of six sentences. You should try these before moving on to the First Certificate level Exam Exercises. In each exercise, one of the six sentences is correct. Answers and notes are on pages 57 and 58.

1   I lost some money on my way to home.
2   She is much more intelligent than you imagine.
3   They had not been looking for no gold.
4   He went to his room and has read the newspaper there.
5   The doctor has been visited his patients.
6   I would not lend to him any money.

1   We decided to go to London by a train.
2   Are you being ready to go out yet?
3   He learnt to drive last week and had bought a car this week.
4   She was not keen on going really to university.
5   On the whole I thought it was quite a good play.
6   I managed to sell less six tickets.

1   My little brother made a toy castle out of wood and plastic.
2   Her friends all sent for a letter to the newspaper.
3   She never heard nothing all night.
4   He saved his money in order for to buy a car.
5   I had begun studying Biology when I was 14 years of old.
6   My brother put a scarf on himself before going out.

1   We eventually found a shop which selling perfume.
2   The library was been built in 1925.
3   My mother lent the book to one of our neighbours.
4   John has plenty of the wine, which he keeps in the cellar.
5   I am being here in England to improve my English.
6   They spent all of day arguing about money.

1   Louise found a few of foreign coins in her pocket.
2   Mike will be going here at nine o'clock in the morning.
3   I know some people who did lived there.
4   I took back my friend home after the party.
5   For the last few weeks I have been really annoyed with John.
6   Jane has finally come up to a decision about her future.

DOING THE EXAM

1   Read through the passage fairly quickly to get a general idea of what the passage is about. Do not begin looking for mistakes yet.

2   Now read through the passage more carefully looking for extra words this time. Some mistakes will be more obvious than others. Write down on the answer sheet any mistakes which you have found.

3   Read the lines in which you have not found a mistake again. If you find a mistake, write it down on the answer sheet.

4   When you are sure you have found all the mistakes, put in the ticks (✓) for the correct lines.

Remember

• There will never be more than one mistake in a line, so *never* write more than one word for each answer.

• If a word appears more than once in a line, it is not the wrong word.

- If a word is wrong in one line, it will not be wrong in another line.
- There will usually not be more than 5 correct lines. If you think there are more than 5 correct lines, look carefully again at those lines which you think are correct.
- There will *usually* be at least 3 correct lines. If you have found fewer than 3 correct lines, look carefully through the passage again.
- If you have found a long series of correct lines all together (e.g. more than three), it is probably a good idea to look at these lines more closely as there may well be a mistake in one of them. Examiners may at times put several correct lines together (see the Exam Exercises) but usually the correct lines are in different parts of the passage.
- When you copy out a word which is wrong, make sure you spell it correctly.
- If you change your mind about an answer, rub it out and write in the new answer. (If you put an answer in brackets or put a line through it, it is not always clear that you want this answer to be ignored.)
- When you have decided which lines are correct, remember to put a tick (✓). If you simply leave the answer space blank, the examiner will think that you have missed out this answer and will not give you a mark for it.

EXAM EXERCISES

The four Exam Exercises which follow are not in order of difficulty. All of them are at First Certificate level, along with the instructions from the examination:

Read the text and look carefully at each line. Some of the lines are correct and some have a word which should not be there.

If a line is correct, put a tick (✓) by the number **on the separate answer sheet**. If a line has a word which should **not** be there, write the word **on the separate answer sheet**. There are two examples at the beginning of each text (**0** and **00**).

**EXAM
EXERCISE 1**

Examples:

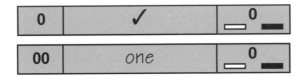

A MISSING DOG

  0 My husband and I were very worried last week when our dog,
 00 Brandy, went missing on one Saturday. It was a beautiful day and
  1 we spent most the afternoon sitting in the garden. Brandy was with
  2 us although we did not pay much attention to him. Later, we went
  3 into the house for having a cup of tea and suddenly realised that
  4 Brandy was nowhere to be seen. We went back into the garden and
  5 called at him but he did not appear. We began to feel anxious as we
  6 live on a busy road and never let Brandy go out on to the road
  7 without one us. We set off to look for him. Half an hour later we
  8 were back home not having seen nothing of Brandy. I was about to
  9 phone the police to ask if there might had been any accidents
 10 involving some dogs when there was a knock at the door; it was the
 11 old lady who lives at next door. She had Brandy with her. He had

12 wandered back into her house earlier and she had given him
13 something to eat. Unfortunately, she had closed the door, had fallen
14 fast asleep and not heard us calling Brandy. Although we had felt
15 rather annoyed with her, our main feeling was one of a great relief.

Answers and notes on page 59.

Please read the instructions above Exam Exercise 1 on page 30.

**EXAM
EXERCISE 2**

0	*the*	__ **0** __
00	✓	__ **0** __

Examples:

A DIFFICULT JOURNEY

 0 I had the dreadful problems getting to work last Thursday morning
00 because of the weather. Normally I walk to the railway station
 1 which is about one kilometre from my house and then catch a train
 2 into town. When I woke up on Thursday, I saw that it was snowing
 3 heavily and realised that I would have to leave early. I did not
 4 bother to have any breakfast but put on me some warm clothes and
 5 set off for work. The snow was really too thick on the ground and
 6 made my walking very difficult. I slipped and fell on three
 7 occasions but, fortunately, did not hurt myself very greatly. When I
 8 reached at the station, I thought I would have missed the train but,
 9 although I was almost half of an hour late, the train had not yet
10 arrived. An hour later I was on the point of going back to home
11 when the train had finally arrived. I got on the train but it remained
12 in the station for another twenty minutes yet. Eventually it started
13 but it had to keep on stopping every few minutes because of the
14 snow. I arrived at work feeling really tired and annoyed; the
15 journey, which normally takes me less forty minutes, had taken over
    three hours.

Answers and notes on page 59.

Please read the instructions above Exam Exercise 1 on page 30.

**EXAM
EXERCISE 3**

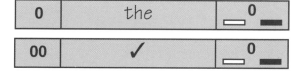

0	*the*	__ **0** __
00	✓	__ **0** __

Examples:

AN EMBARRASSING EXPERIENCE

 0 One of my friends, Jane Barker, had an embarrassing experience the
00 last year when she was on holiday abroad with her husband, Peter. On
 1 the final evening of the holiday, they decided to have look round the
 2 various restaurants in town until they found one which really appealed

3 to them. They set off just little after seven o'clock and eventually came
4 across an attractive restaurant in the old part of town. They decided to
5 go in as they thought that the prices were not too high up and as there
6 was a choice of those traditional dishes. The meal was really
7 delicious and they thoroughly enjoyed it. Everything went just well
8 until the waiter has brought the bill. Peter put his hand in his pocket
9 to get his wallet and suddenly realised that he had left it back at the
10 hotel. Jane had no money on her at all. They explained what had
11 happened them to the manager. He was very annoyed but, after a
12 while, he allowed Peter to go back to the hotel to get hold his wallet.
13 However, he insisted that Jane must had to stay beside him until Peter
14 returned. Jane had to wait for well over an hour – she told to me that it
15 was the most embarrassing hour of her life and that she would never go
out without money again.

Answers and notes on page 60.

EXAM EXERCISE 4

Please read the instructions above Exam Exercise 1 on page 30.

Examples:

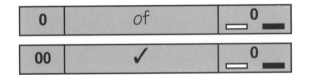

A VISIT TO STRATFORD

0 Last week I spent a most enjoyable few of days at Stratford-upon-
00 Avon with three of my friends. We decided to go several weeks
1 ago and I have booked rooms for the four of us at a hotel in the
2 town. The hotel was really impressive on the outside but the
3 bedrooms were rather small. We were quite late for arriving on the
4 first evening as we had been at work during the whole of day and
5 all which we wanted to do then was to have a good meal and go to
6 our bed. The following morning we got up quite late and ate a
7 large breakfast in the hotel. We spent the rest of the day by driving
8 round the countryside, stopping each now and again to go for short
9 walks. On the second day there we managed to get tickets for the
10 theatre and went to watch at one of Shakespeare's plays in the
11 evening. Earlier in the day two of my friends had said me that they
12 would rather to spend the evening at a pub, but in fact we all
13 thoroughly enjoyed the play and then went to the pub afterwards. I
14 saw a woman there whom I thought I had recognised – I suddenly
15 realised that then she was one of the actresses from the play.

Answers and notes on page 60.

LOOKING AT THE EXAM

This part of the Use of English paper is a word-building test; this means that you are given a word from which you have to make a new word.

In the exam you have a passage to read in which there are eleven empty spaces. At the end of every line you will find a word from which you have to make another word which correctly fills the empty space in that line. As in the earlier parts of the paper, the first missing word has the figure **0** in front of it and is an example.

Sometimes, as in Part 4, there will be an extra line at the bottom of the passage which does not have an empty space and a number. Again, this line is there because it has not been possible to write the whole of the passage in the eleven lines. This line is not part of the test and there is no new word to be formed here. The questions in Part 5 are numbered 56–65.

FILLING IN THE ANSWER SHEET

In this part of the exam you simply have to write the answer in the appropriate place on the answer sheet. Obviously, you must spell the word correctly. As in other parts of the paper, it is better to print the word in capital letters rather than to use your normal handwriting so as to make sure that the person marking the paper can tell if your spelling is correct. If, because of your writing, it is not clear whether or not your spelling is correct, you will not be given a mark. Remember again that you must write only *one* word on the answer sheet; if you write more than one word, you will not be given a mark.

Below is an example of a line from a passage which could be used in one of these tests:

    John said that he had a new **(1)** ..... who came from America.   TEACH

The new word has to be made from *teach*. The answer is, of course, *teacher*, so that is the word you would write on your answer sheet.

Make sure you do not write in the last colum of the answer sheet, marked **Do not write here**.

WORDS TO BE FORMED

The words to be formed will usually be nouns*, verbs*, adjectives* or adverbs*. Sometimes you will need to change the word you are given once in order to form the new word. Here are two examples of this:

    visit   →   *visitor*
    quick   →   *quickly*

At other times, though, you may have to change the word twice in order to form the new word. Here are two examples of this:

    own   →   *owner*   →   *ownership*
    fright   →   *frighten*   →   *frightened*

Sometimes you will form the new word by adding something to the beginning of the word you have been given. Here are two examples:

    appear   →   *disappear*
    sleep   →   *asleep*

More often, though, you will form the new word by adding something to the end of the word you have been given. Here are two examples:

    sad   →   *sadness*
    grow   →   *growth*

Occasionally you will form the new word by changing the word from the middle. Here are six examples of this type of change:

long	→	*length*
strong	→	*strength*
deep	→	*depth*
broad	→	*breadth*
pride	→	*proud*

You may quite often have to change an adjective* into an adverb*. Usually to do this you simply add *-ly* to the end of the word you have been given.

slow	→	*slowly*
quiet	→	*quietly*

However, remember the two following rules:
If an adjective ends in *-y*, to form the adverb change *-y* to *-ily*.
If an adjective ends in *-l*, to form the adverb change *-l* to *-lly*.

happy	→	*happily*
hopeful	→	*hopefully*

Usually, but not always, the new word which you form will be longer than the word that you have been given.

READING THE PASSAGE

Sometimes when you see the word which you have to change, you may think immediately that you know what it has to be changed into. However, the words can usually be changed in more than one way and so it is important that you read the passage to make sure that you know how to change the word. For instance if you see that the word you have to change is *enjoy*, you may immediately think that it should be changed to *enjoyable*. This may not be the case. For example, if you had to form a word from *enjoy* in the following sentence

It was a day of total (1) ..... for everyone who was there.

then the word to be formed would be *enjoyment*. If you do not read the passage carefully, you may well form the wrong word from the word you have been given.

To help you think about the different new words that can be formed from a word you have been given, there is a list of ten words below. Write down two words that can be formed from each of the words on the list. (In some cases more than two words can be formed.) Answers and notes are on page 61.

New words
1 succeed
2 manage
3 translate
4 please
5 origin
6 consider
7 follow
8 soft
9 shop
10 belief

PLURALS*

Sometimes when you have to form a noun*, you will have to put the noun in the plural. When this happens, make sure that you do write the plural form of the word (normally by adding *-s*). The signs that tell you that you must use a plural form of a noun are a following verb in the plural (e.g. *are*, *were*, *have*) or words such as *many*, *several*, *some*, *(a) few*, *a lot of* in front of the noun. Often when the words *a* or *the* are not with the noun, that noun will be in the plural.

Below are six short sentences. Change the word at the end of the line into the suitable word to fill the empty space. In all cases the words which you form are nouns in the plural. Think what it is which indicates that the word must be in the plural. Answers and notes are on page 61.

1 Both my brothers want to be **(1)** ..... .   ENGINE
2 The firm has already made several **(2)** ..... to its main building.   EXTEND
3 Her **(3)** ..... of the country were very mixed.   IMPRESS
4 **(4)** ..... with the machine keep happening.   DIFFICULT
5 Three of the **(5)** ..... had accidents.   CYCLE
6 The **(6)** ..... think he should go to court.   LAW

NEGATIVES*

Sometimes you will need to use a negative form of a noun*, verb*, adjective* or adverb*. These are often formed by putting *-un*, *-im*, *-in*, *-il*, *-ir*, or *-dis* at the front of a word, or by putting *-less* at the end of the word. What is the negative form of these words? The answers are given on page 61.

1 probable
2 responsible
3 usual
4 obey
5 legally
6 certainty
7 helpful
8 correct
9 likely
10 embark

When you read the passage in this test, it will sometimes indicate that a negative form of the given word is needed. Look at this example.

John's father accused him of **(1)** ..... .   HONEST

If you look only at the word you are given and do not read the sentence with any care, you will probably guess that the answer is *honesty*. However, if you read the sentence more carefully, you will know that when you accuse a person of something, you are criticising that person. You are not likely to criticise a person for a good quality such as honesty and so the negative form of *honesty* is needed. (The correct answer is *dishonesty*.)

In the ten sentences which follow, all the words which you must supply are negative words. Write down the words and also think what it is in the sentence which makes a negative word necessary. The answers are on page 61.

1 I was **(1)** ..... to concentrate because of all the noise.   ABLE
2 Jean is so kind that it is **(2)** ..... to be angry with her for long.   POSSIBLE
3 He was **(3)** ..... to help because he had so much work to do.   WILLING
4 I find John really awkward as he **(4)** ..... with everything I say.   AGREE
5 She became increasingly **(5)** ..... with her lazy husband.   PATIENT
6 People complained because John was **(6)** ..... dressed.   SUITABLE

7 The film was so **(7)** ..... that I fell asleep.   INTEREST
8 The boy wanted to show he was **(8)** ..... of his parents.   DEPENDENT
9 It was very **(9)** ..... of you to break that cup.   CARE
10 It is **(10)** ..... for me to see you today as I am very busy.   CONVENIENT

PRACTICE EXERCISES

Below are four practice exercises of ten sentences each for you to work through before
beginning the full Exam Exercises. They will help you to get used to doing this sort of test and
to reach the First Certificate standard.

In all the exercises, use the word given in capitals at the end of the line to form a word that fits in
the space in the same line. The answers and notes are on page 62.

PRACTICE EXERCISE 1

1 He worked as a **(1)** ..... before he retired.   BAKE
2 We were delighted by the **(2)** ..... of their welcome.   WARM
3 I am afraid that Peter lacks qualities of **(3)** ..... .   LEADER
4 I'll **(4)** ..... be rather late tomorrow.   PROBABLE
5 The **(5)** ..... for the wedding are almost complete.   PREPARE
6 We had a really **(6)** ..... holiday.   WONDER
7 Helen showed me great **(7)** ..... when I really needed it.   KIND
8 When driving, you should always consider the **(8)** ..... of others. SAFE
9 **(9)** ..... , the film had almost finished by the time we arrived.   FORTUNATE
10 His uncle is a very **(10)** ..... man.   WEALTH

PRACTICE EXERCISE 2

1 I was very **(1)** ..... after walking so far.   THIRST
2 He has to put a lot of sugar in his tea to **(2)** ..... it.   SWEET
3 She shows great **(3)** ..... to succeed.   DETERMINE
4 Louise is **(4)** ..... very polite.   GENERAL
5 That old washing machine is completely **(5)** ..... now.   USE
6 Sarah gave in her **(6)** ..... without having another job to go to. RESIGN
7 I can never take Jim **(7)** ..... .   SERIOUS
8 The government **(8)** ..... are coming to the factory on Tuesday. INSPECT
9 Tony says he would rather be **(9)** ..... than live in that dirty flat. HOME
10 She was **(10)** ..... not to have been knocked down by the lorry. LUCK

PRACTICE EXERCISE 3

1 We saw a really **(1)** ..... play last week.   FUN
2 There is a **(2)** ..... for the boys in this group to be lazy.   TEND
3 Paul was knocked **(3)** ..... when the man hit him.   CONSCIOUS
4 It is very **(4)** ..... to cross that road at night.   DANGER
5 The manager spoke to all the workers **(5)** ..... .   INDIVIDUAL
6 My sister suffers from **(6)** ..... when she is away from home. LONELY
7 Mary said the weather was going to turn **(7)** ..... this afternoon. STORM
8 People from many different **(8)** ..... attended the conference. ORGANISE
9 They decided to take out extra **(9)** ..... on their house.   INSURE
10 He hopes to gain extra **(10)** ..... by studying at night school. QUALIFY

1 There were three **(1)** ..... standing at the door.
2 Catherine is **(2)** ..... recognised as an expert on plants.
3 Bob would love to be a **(3)** ..... footballer.
4 It is not my **(4)** ..... to see that all the doors are locked.
5 I think it is **(5)** ..... that I will be able to go to Ireland next year.
6 The building is **(6)** ..... older than it appears.
7 She was not satisfied with the **(7)** ..... she received at hospital.
8 My cousin has real **(8)** ..... ability.
9 He was very hot and began to **(9)** ..... his shirt.
10 Claire **(10)** ..... everything her father tells her.

STRANGE
WIDE
PROFESSION
RESPONSIBLE
DOUBT
CONSIDER
TREAT
ART
DO
BELIEF

DOING THE EXAM

1 Read through the passage to get an idea of what it is about. Do not try to form new words yet.

2 Read the passage as far as the example **(0)** and look at the word which has been formed.

3 Read the passage as far as the first empty space **(56)** and look at the word you have been given. Keeping in mind what the passage is about, try to form the correct new word.

4 When you have decided what the new word is, write it on the answer sheet by the number for that space. If you cannot decide what the word is, leave this item and move on to the next empty space.

5 Make sure that you spell the answer correctly and that your writing is clear.

6 Do the same for all 10 empty spaces.

7 When you have decided on the correct word for the final space **(65)**, go back to any of the items which you have not filled in. Try again to decide what the missing word is. If in the end you really have no idea of the answer, write any word on the answer sheet which seems to be based on the word you have been given. There is always a chance that it might be right.

8 When you are working through this part of the test, there may be times when you are fairly sure of the correct answer but feel that you would like to look at the item again later. If this happens, write the word which you think is correct on the answer sheet and put an asterisk (*) or some other kind of mark by the word you are given on the question paper. This will remind you to look at the item later. *Do not put this asterisk on the answer sheet.*

9 If you do return to one of the items mentioned in number 7 above and you decide to change the answer, rub out the answer you first thought of and then write in the answer which you now think is correct.

Remember

• Write only *one* word for each answer. If you write more than one word, you will not get a mark.

• If you miss out an answer, make sure that when you put in the next answer, you put it by the correct number (that is to say that if, for example, you missed out answer 57, do not put the answer for 58 at the side of number 57).

• If you change your mind about an answer, remember to rub out the answer you had already indicated.

• Always write in an answer even if you have no idea what the correct answer is. It is better to make a guess than to leave an answer blank.

EXAM EXERCISES

The four exam exercises which follow are not in order of difficulty. All of them are at First Certificate level.

EXAM EXERCISE 1

Read the text below. Use the word given in capitals at the end of each line to form a word that fits in the space in the same line. There is an example at the beginning **(0)**.

Example:

0	recently	0

A NEW SHOP

A new shop has **(0)** ..... opened in the centre of town selling a	RECENT
wide **(1)** ..... of clothes for both men and women. The shop is	SELECT
owned by an **(2)** ..... young couple from Australia. All the	ENERGY
clothes on sale are extremely **(3)** ..... and are displayed in a most	FASHION
(4) ..... manner. However, it has to be admitted that prices are	ATTRACT
rather high and, **(5)** ..... , this means that many people looking in	FORTUNATE
the window and seeing how **(6)** ..... the clothes are will not go in	EXPENSE
the shop. This is a great pity since it is a real **(7)** ..... to be in the	PLEASE
shop as the staff are so **(8)** ..... ; they are always very patient and	HELP
willing to give **(9)** ..... without putting any pressure on the	ADVISE
customer to buy. The shop certainly deserves to **(10)**	SUCCESS

Answers and notes on page 63.

EXAM EXERCISE 2

Read the text below. Use the word given in capitals at the end of each line to form a word that fits in the space in the same line. There is an example at the beginning **(0)**.

Example:

0	amazement	0

A LION ON THE STREETS OF LONDON

A few years ago there was considerable **(0)** ..... at a police	AMAZE
station in a **(1)** ..... suburb of north London when a number of	PEACE
local **(2)** ..... reported seeing a young lion jumping over garden	RESIDE
fences. The lion was said to be about 75 centimetres in **(3)**	LONG
Thirty police officers, a helicopter and a **(4)** ..... from London	SCIENCE
Zoo joined in a search for the animal. When it was **(5)**	EVENTUAL
found, it turned out to be nothing more **(6)** ..... than a large	DANGER
brown cat which was fast **(7)** ..... on the lawn of its house. The	SLEEP
cat's **(8)** ..... said that it was an extremely timid creature and that	OWN
it was very **(9)** ..... for it to leave the garden. For some reason	USUAL
or other, it had decided to explore the **(10)** ..... that morning.	NEIGHBOUR

Answers and notes on page 63.

Read the text below. Use the word given in capitals at the end of each line to form a word that fits in the space in the same line. There is an example at the beginning (0).

Example: | 0 | *directors* | 0 |

NEW JOBS FOR BRIDSEA

The (0) ..... of Walton's Watches have announced that, as a result of a large (1) ..... in their business overseas, it is their intention to carry out a major (2) ..... of their factory in Bridsea in order to cope with increased demand. A (3) ..... has been made for work to begin (4) ..... on building an extension to the existing factory in the centre of Bridsea. Although it is (5) ..... that (6) ..... will begin before the end of the year, people wishing to work for this highly (7) ..... company should contact John Payne, the Personnel (8) ..... , as soon as possible. The company is looking for (9) ..... people of all ages who are keen to make a positive (10) .... to the future of the company.

DIRECT
IMPROVE
EXPAND
DECIDE
IMMEDIATE
LIKELY
PRODUCE
SUCCESS
MANAGE
ENTHUSIASM
CONTRIBUTE

Answers and notes on page 63.

Read the text below. Use the word given in capitals at the end of each line to form a word that fits in the space in the same line. There is an example at the beginning (0).

Example: | 0 | *inventions* | 0 |

MOBILE PHONES

One of the (0) ..... of the late twentieth century which has become (1) ..... important is the mobile phone, that is the phone that you can carry with you. When they first went on (2) ..... , the phones were very large and heavy and extremely (3) ..... , but now the price has fallen and they can (4) ..... be carried in a pocket as they are so light and slim. The phones are (5) ..... for people who travel a lot as without the phone it would be (6) ..... for them to stay in touch with the office. It is, however, (7) ..... if you are on a train looking forward to a (8) ..... journey and somebody begins talking (9) ..... on a mobile phone, often, it seems, about nothing of any great (10) ..... .

INVENT
INCREASE
SELL
EXPENSE
EASY
USE
POSSIBLE
ANNOY
PEACE
LOUD
IMPORTANT

Answers and notes on page 63.

Trial Paper A

You have 1 hour and 15 minutes in which to complete this test.

PART 1

For questions **1-15**, read the text below and decide which answer **A**, **B**, **C** or **D** best fits each space. Use only **one** word in each space. There is an example at the beginning **(0)**.

Write your answer (**A**, **B**, **C** or **D**) **on the separate answer sheet**.

Example:

| 0 | **A** moment | **B** season | **C** time | **D** session |

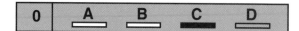

THE NUMBER 13

Arnold Schönberg was born in Austria in 1874. For a **(0)** ..... he worked in a bank as his family had financial problems following the death of his father, but eventually he achieved his real **(1)** ..... which was to become a composer.

It is well-known that many people find it extremely difficult to **(2)** ..... Schönberg's music. It is less well-known that Schönberg was absolutely terrified of the number thirteen. He was born on 13th September and considered that this **(3)** ..... that the number thirteen would be unlucky for him. His **(4)** ..... of the number became so great that he began to be worried by **(5)** ..... number that could be **(6)** ..... by 13. He became **(7)** ..... that he would die on his sixty-fifth birthday as sixty-five is the number **(8)** ..... when five is multiplied by thirteen. In fact Schönberg **(9)** ..... on until 1951, when he was seventy-six; this did not **(10)** ..... him until somebody mentioned that if you add seven and six together you get thirteen. This was **(11)** ..... else for him to **(12)** ..... about but he told his friends that if he **(13)** ..... to live until his **(14)** ..... birthday, he would be **(15)** ..... for some time. Sadly, he died later that year – it was on the thirteenth day of the month.

1	**A** job	**B** passion	**C** employment	**D** ambition
2	**A** listen	**B** know	**C** hear	**D** understand
3	**A** predicted	**B** said	**C** meant	**D** assured
4	**A** suffering	**B** fear	**C** problem	**D** anxiety
5	**A** any	**B** the	**C** some	**D** all
6	**A** increased	**B** divided	**C** split	**D** expanded
7	**A** informed	**B** aware	**C** convinced	**D** conscious
8	**A** resulted	**B** produced	**C** arrived	**D** shown
9	**A** continued	**B** passed	**C** kept	**D** lived
10	**A** bother	**B** notice	**C** confuse	**D** displease
11	**A** another	**B** anything	**C** more	**D** something
12	**A** worry	**B** upset	**C** care	**D** trouble
13	**A** proceeded	**B** could	**C** managed	**D** carried
14	**A** future	**B** succeeding	**C** last	**D** next
15	**A** right	**B** safe	**C** sparing	**D** lively

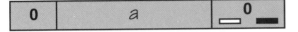

For questions **16-30**, read the text below and think of the word which best fits each space. Use only **one** word in each space. There is an example at the beginning **(0)**.

Write your word **on the separate answer sheet.**

Example:

0	*a*	0

FROM BALINE TO BERLIN

Israel Baline was the youngest child in **(0)** ..... poor family that had moved from Russia to America in 1893. Money was **(16)** ..... scarce that even the small amount of money that Israel earned **(17)** ..... a child on the streets of New York from selling newspapers was important for the family.

One evening, **(18)** ..... sold all his newspapers, Israel was sitting on a bridge beside the East river **(19)** ..... a crane which was unloading coal **(20)** ..... a boat hit him and knocked him into the river. He **(21)** ..... probably have drowned if it had not been **(22)** ..... a man who jumped into the river and rescued him. Israel was taken to hospital **(23)** ..... the doctors found that he **(24)** ..... still holding the few pennies he **(25)** ..... earned that day.

As he grew older, Israel discovered that he had a talent for writing songs. Realising that his name **(26)** ..... not sound very American, he changed **(27)** ..... to Irving Berlin and went on to compose some of the most popular songs of the twentieth century. In **(28)** ..... of his poor beginnings, he **(29)** ..... a rich and famous man when he died in 1989, **(30)** ..... the age of 101.

PART 3

For questions **31-40**, complete the second sentence so that it has a similar meaning to the first sentence, using the word given. **Do not change the word given.** You must use between two and five words, including the word given. There is an example at the beginning **(0)**. Write **only** the missing words **on the separate answer sheet**.

Example:

0   Louise really likes classical music.
   keen
   Louise .... classical music.

The gap can be filled by the words 'is really keen on' so you write:

0	*is really keen on*

31   He was sorry to miss the film
   missed

   He wished .... the film.

32 Janet has difficulty in walking far.
   difficult

   Janet .... far.

33 There are not as many flowers this year as last year.
   flowers

   There .... last year than there are this year.

34 My brother said, "I will be leaving at two o'clock".
   he

   My brother said that .... at two o'clock.

35 They did not reply so I did not know if they were coming to the wedding.
   replied

   If they .... known if they were coming to the wedding.

36 My father worked at the airport and had to examine passports.
   responsible

   My father worked at the airport and .... passports.

37 It is possible to see Liverpool from the top of that hill.
   be

   Liverpool .... from the top of that hill.

38 They could not understand the Italian boy because they did not speak Italian.
   able

   If they .... Italian, they could have understood the Italian boy.

39 My friend had very little to eat this morning.
   not

   My friend .... to eat this morning.

40 All the shops were closed yesterday apart from the chemist's.
   that

   The chemist's was the .... open yesterday.

For questions **41-55**, read the text below and look carefully at each line. Some of the lines are correct, and some have a word which should not be there.

If the line is correct, put a tick (✓) by the number **on the separate answer sheet**. If a line has a word which should **not** be there, write the word **on the separate answer sheet**. There are two examples at the beginning (**0** and **00**).

Examples:

0	✓	0
00	*can*	0

AN INVITATION

0   I have been wondering if you would like to come and spend a couple

00 of weeks at my house this summer. We can have a spare room in

41 the house which is always been used for guests so there will be no

42 problem in putting you up. The best time when to come would be in

43 August since that the weather is usually good then and we would be

44 able to get out quite often. There is a large castle at about twenty

45 kilometres from the house and if that would be interest you we could

46 easily go there. As you know it, I live in a fairly small village and

47 you might think that there would not be much to do, but, in fact, it

48 is a very lively place, especially in the summer when there are

49 always plenty of these things going on. I do not think you will be

50 bored off. One of the most enjoyable of the summer events is an

51 international jazz festival which takes its place in the middle of

52 August and lasts for over than a week. The festival attracts people

53 coming from all over the word and is always great fun. Do let me

54 to know if and when you can come so that I can begin making plans

55 for your stay as soon as possible.

PART 5

For questions **56-65**, read the text below. Use the word given in capitals at the end of each line to form a word that fits in the space in the same line. There is an example at the beginning **(0)**. Write your word **on the separate answer sheet.**

Example:

00	waiting	0

FIRE AT THE STATION

A fire broke out yesterday afternoon in the **(0)** ..... room at	WAIT
Brenton railway station. **(56)** ..... , the fire brigade were on the	LUCK
scene almost **(57)** ..... and were able to prevent flames from	IMMEDIATE
spreading to other **(58)** ..... on the station. Although several	BUILD
people had been in the room, there were no serious **(59)**	INJURE
Several trains had to be cancelled but a normal **(60)** ..... was	SERVE
back in **(61)** ..... by the end of the afternoon. Peter Williamson,	OPERATE
the **(62)** ..... manager for the railways, said that, fortunately,	REGION
damage to the station was not great. A full **(63)** ..... into the	INVESTIGATE
cause of the fire is being carried out, although as yet it is **(64)**	POSSIBLE
to say with any degree of **(65)** ..... exactly how it started.	CERTAIN

Answers and notes for Trial Paper A are on pages 64 and 65.

You have 1 hour and 15 minutes in which to complete this test.

PART 1

For questions **1-15**, read the text below and decide which answer **A**, **B**, **C** or **D** best fits each space.
Use only **one** word in each space. There is an example at the beginning **(0)**.
Write your answer (**A**, **B**, **C** or **D**) **on the separate answer sheet**.

Example:

0   **A** visions   **B** appearances   **C** looks   **D** sights

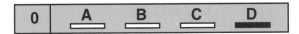

THE STATUE OF LIBERTY

One of the most impressive **(0)** ..... of New York, indeed of America, is the Statue of Liberty.

The statue **(1)** ..... at the entrance to New York harbour, just a **(2)** ..... distance from Manhattan island. It is about 50 metres in **(3)** ..... and is of a woman holding in one hand a torch, and in the other a book bearing the words *4th July 1776*, the **(4)** ..... on which America gained her independence.

The statue was not, in fact, **(5)** ..... for by Americans but was a **(6)** ..... from the people of France to **(7)** ..... the one hundredth anniversary of America's independence. It was **(8)** ..... designed by Gustave Eiffel, the man who also designed the Eiffel Tower in Paris. The statue was **(9)** .... in France and was then pulled into **(10)** ..... so that it could be sent conveniently to America by ship.

It is **(11)** ..... impressive to see the statue, whether one is arriving in New York after a long sea voyage or if one is simply **(12)** ..... a short sightseeing trip from nearby Battery Park. However, for the millions who in the past had crossed the Atlantic in **(13)** .... of a better life, often having had to **(14)** ..... with awful conditions for weeks on board ship, the statue must have been a wonderful symbol of **(15)** ..... for the future.

1	**A** raises	**B** stands	**C** dwells	**D** situates
2	**A** brief	**B** long	**C** short	**D** far
3	**A** long	**B** height	**C** length	**D** high
4	**A** period	**B** year	**C** date	**D** time
5	**A** paid	**B** requested	**C** demanded	**D** bought
6	**A** reward	**B** support	**C** favour	**D** gift
7	**A** rejoice	**B** enjoy	**C** remark	**D** celebrate
8	**A** somehow	**B** largely	**C** somewhat	**D** greatly
9	**A** set	**B** done	**C** built	**D** formed
10	**A** parts	**B** shapes	**C** pieces	**D** sections
11	**A** most	**B** yet	**C** already	**D** ever
12	**A** taking	**B** spending	**C** sailing	**D** going
13	**A** longing	**B** search	**C** desire	**D** aim
14	**A** join in	**B** keep up	**C** get in	**D** put up
15	**A** hope	**B** faith	**C** joy	**D** success

PART 2

For questions **16-30**, read the text below and think of the word which best fits each space. Use only **one** word in each space. There is an example at the beginning **(0)**.

Write your word **on the separate answer sheet**.

Example:

0	*do*	0

NOT TELLING THE WHOLE TRUTH

Sometimes when we speak to other people we **(0)** ..... not tell them the whole truth but tell them what we think they want to hear. Helen, **(16)** ..... research student at an American university, gave an example of this **(17)** ..... she returned home for her sister's wedding. At the reception, she talked to relatives and old school-friends, all of **(18)** ..... wanted to know how she was getting **(19)** ..... . She had no intention of **(20)** ..... lies, yet after several conversations she felt that she **(21)** ..... not told the whole truth.

In some conversations she told people how well she **(22)** ..... doing, how much she enjoyed her research, and how she had made **(23)** ..... of new friends. However, in other conversations she spoke of **(24)** ..... to work long hours, of how she had very **(25)** ..... money and of how she disliked the cheap accommodation she had to **(26)** ..... in.

She later realised that she had given her parents and relatives a very positive picture of her life so that they would not worry **(27)** ..... her. However, she knew that many of her friends were in dull, boring jobs, and as she **(28)** ..... not want to make **(29)** ..... jealous of her, she gave a much **(30)** ..... negative description. Both descriptions were true, but she told the different people only what she thought would please them.

PART 3

For questions **31-40**, complete the second sentence so that it has a similar meaning to the first sentence, using the word given. **Do not change the word given.** You must use between two and five words, including the word given. There is an example at the beginning **(0)**. Write only the missing words **on the separate answer sheet**.

Example:

    0   Louise really likes classical music.
            keen
            Louise .... classical music.

The gap can be filled by the words 'is really keen on' so you write:

0	is really keen on

31 I knew nobody at the lecture last night.
    not

    I .... at the lecture last night.

32 The soldier asked for permission to return home.
    he

    The soldier asked .... return home.

33 Mrs Hyde said that she was sorry she had arrived too late for the meeting.
    apologised

    Mrs Hyde .... too late for the meeting.

34 It took the garage mechanic less than ten minutes to repair the car.
    car

    The garage mechanic .... less than ten minutes.

35 They would have caught the train but for the fog this morning.
    it

    They would have caught the train if .... this morning.

36 That is the best book I have ever read.
    book

    I have never read .... than that one.

37 "Will you help me with the decorating?" my brother asked.
    help

    My brother asked me if .... with the decorating.

38 My little sister does not save any of her money but wastes it all on sweets.
    instead

    My little sister wastes all her money on sweets .... some of it.

39 Sally has been working at the factory for a year.
    year

    It .... Sally began working at the factory.

40 We were so tired that we did not go to the theatre.
    not

    We would have gone to the theatre .... so tired.

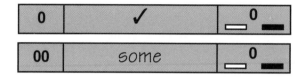

For questions **41-45**, read the text below and look carefully at each line. Some of the lines are correct, and some have a word which should not be there.

If the line is correct, put a tick (✓) by the number **on the separate answer sheet**. If a line has a word which should **not** be there, write the word **on the separate answer sheet**. There are two examples at the beginning (**0** and **00**).

Examples:

0	✓	___0___
00	*some*	___0___

A SHOPPING TRIP

  0 Something which I have always disliked doing is shopping for

00 some clothes and I avoid doing this for as long as possible.

41 However, last week I realised that I would have to go buy myself

42 a new coat for winter as the one that I have no longer fits on me.

43 This is probably not too surprising as it is at the least eight years

44 since I have bought it. I went into town on the bus and looked in

45 the window of a very smart clothes shop but decided that the

46 prices were far more dearer than I could afford. Nearby there

47 was another clothes shop where the prices were more reasonable.

48 I tried on several coats there but none of them suited to me. I left

49 the shop and, feeling hungry, I went to a café where I had bought

50 to myself a sandwich and a cup of tea. Just opposite the café was

51 found a large bookshop which I could not resist. I went in and

52 was there for long over an hour as there were so many books

53 which caught my attention. I ended up buying four books which

54 were being of particular interest to me. I forgot all about the coat

55 I had been intended to buy as I was so keen to begin reading the

     books that I went straight back home.

PART 5

For questions **56-65**, read the text below. Use the word given in capitals at the end of each line to form a word that fits in the space in the same line. There is an example at the beginning **(0)**. Write your word **on the separate answer sheet**.

Example:

0	celebrations	0

VILLAGE FOOTBALL

There were **(0)** ..... taking place in the village of Haydon last night   CELEBRATE

following the local football team's **(56)** ..... victory over the   IMPRESS

neighbouring village of Watley. The match, held **(57)** ..... for the   ANNUAL

past sixty years, is an event of considerable **(58)** ..... for both   IMPORTANT

villages. Almost all of the **(59)** ..... , including those who normally   INHABIT

show no interest whatsoever in football, turn out to give **(60)** ..... to   ENCOURAGE

their team, which is made up entirely of **(61)** ..... who live in the   PLAY

village. The cup presented to the winners is **(62)** ..... displayed in a   PROUD

village shop throughout the year. There is much **(63)** ..... rivalry   FRIEND

surrounding the match but never any sign of the **(64)** ..... which has   VIOLENT

sometimes spoilt the **(65)** ..... game.   PROFESSION

Answers and notes for Trial Paper B are on pages 65 and 66.

Answers and Notes

2 PART 1: MULTIPLE CHOICE CLOZE

All answers in this part of the paper are worth **1 mark.**

PRACTICE EXERCISE 1
1 **B** live
2 **A** read
3 **B** after
4 **D** well
5 **A** bone

PRACTICE EXERCISE 2
1 **D** job
2 **A** took
3 **C** really
4 **C** forgotten
5 **B** in case

PRACTICE EXERCISE 3
1 **D** be (**Note:** *work* or *qualify* must be followed by *as*)
2 **A** harder

PRACTICE EXERCISE 4
1 **B** past
2 **A** except

PRACTICE EXERCISE 5
1 **A** attending
2 **D** in order

PRACTICE EXERCISE 6
1 **C** because of
2 **A** service

PRACTICE EXERCISE 7
1 **C** end
2 **A** serving (**Note:** *with* after *customers* means that only *serving* is possible)
3 **C** offer (**Note:** *sale* is tempting but it is *meat* that is on sale, not *prices*)

PRACTICE EXERCISE 8
1 **D** spending
2 **A** enjoyed
3 **B** save (**Note:** *collect* suggests that the person is asking people for money)

PRACTICE EXERCISE 9
1 **A** feeling
2 **C** reason
3 **C** damage

PRACTICE EXERCISE 10
1 **D** time
2 **B** waste
3 **C** since

No longer a secret

1 **A** occasion
2 **B** a notice (**Note:** *announcements* are usually heard, not seen)
3 **D** served (**Note:** *presented* and *provided* must be followed by *with*)
4 **A** along with (**Note:** *as well* must be followed by *as; in addition* must be followed by *to*)
5 **C** came (**Note:** as *with* is present, *carried* and *brought* cannot be correct)
6 **D** bill
7 **C** want
8 **B** part
9 **B** called (**Note:** *stayed* suggests that they spent at least one night at the farm; as *at* is present, *visited* cannot be correct)
10 **C** impressed
11 **D** approached
12 **C** disappointment
13 **A** stopped
14 **A** appearance
15 **B** let (**Note:** *allow* is tempting but to be correct, it would have to be followed by 'too many people *to* know'.

Exam tip

No. 15 is a good example of why you must read *beyond* the space before deciding on the answer.

Samuel Ireland

1 **C** Knowing (**Note:** *Aware* and *Conscious* must be followed by *of; Finding* must be followed by *out*)
2 **A** decided
3 **C** collected
4 **B** way
5 **D** find
6 **D** interested (**Note:** *interested* is the only one of the words which may be followed by *in*)
7 **A** sent (**Note:** *presented* must be followed by *by*, not *from*.)
8 **D** belonging (**Note:** *kept* and *owned* must be followed by *by*, not *to*)
9 **C** work
10 **C** permission (**Note:** *right* must have *the* in front of it; *allowance* does not have the same meaning as *permission*)

Exam tip

When you are deciding which word is correct, remember to think about *meaning* and *structure*.

---

11 **A** managed
12 **B** failure
13 **D** admitted (**Note:** *admitted* is the only word here that can be followed by the *-ing* form of a verb*)
14 **A** mind (**Note:** *to change one's mind* is a set expression meaning to change one's opinion)
15 **B** remained

EXAM EXERCISE 3

Smoking

1 **A** amount
2 **C** harmful
3 **C** give up
4 **A** link
5 **B** continue
6 **D** helps (**Note:** *helps* is the only word here that does not need *to* in front of a following verb)
7 **C** freedom
8 **B** argued
9 **C** society (**Note:** *society* is the only word here that does not need *the* in front of it)
10 **A** especially
11 **B** encourage
12 **D** present
13 **A** risk (**Note:** *at risk* is a set expression)
14 **D** breathing
15 **B** case

Not saying what we mean

1 **D** so
2 **B** across (**Note:** *to get something across* means *to communicate*)
3 **D** example
4 **B** explained
5 **C** permission
6 **A** tell
7 **A** keen (**Note:** *keen* is the only word here that can be followed by *on*)
8 **D** tone
9 **B** felt
10 **A** simply
11 **D** choice
12 **C** mind (**Note:** *to make up one's mind* is a set expression meaning *to decide*)
13 **B** requests
14 **C** prevented (**Note:** *prevented* is the only word here which has the meaning of making sure that something does not happen)
15 **A** relationship (**Note:** *communication* is not correct because you cannot say *a communication*)

3 PART 2: OPEN CLOZE

All answers in this part of the paper are worth **1 mark**.

PRACTICE EXERCISE 1

1 are (**Note:** *were* is also possible, but less likely)
2 too
3 and
4 their
5 anywhere
6 have
7 what
8 where
9 not
10 would (**Note:** *should* and *could* are possible, but less likely)

1 the
2 than
3 being
4 so
5 was
6 who **or** that
7 though
8 if **or** though
9 enough **or** sufficient
10 anything

1 did
2 it

1 too
2 or

1 the
2 on

1 this
2 where

1 had
2 was
3 few

1 away
2 some
3 for

1 which **or** that
2 Although **or** While
3 will

1 who
2 did
3 when
4 be
5 nobody
6 what
7 were
8 an

EXAM EXERCISE 1

The Isle of Wight

1 one
2 spite
3 between (**Note:** *from* may seem tempting but for this to be correct, the word after *island* would have to be *to,* not *and*)
4 been
5 there
6 which (**Note:** *that* is not possible as the following information is by no means essential to the understanding of *the island*. The words from *which* to *22 kilometres wide* are really extra information; this type of expression is known as a non-defining relative clause.)
7 in
8 for
9 an
10 most (**Note:** the presence of *The* makes *most* the correct word. If the sentence had begun with *A*, then a word such as *very* would have been suitable.)
11 had
12 who (**Note:** *that* is not possible for the same reason as in **6** above; *who* must be used rather than *which*, as the words refer to a person, not a thing.)
13 did
14 his
15 no

Exam tip

Make sure you are familiar with the difference between defining relative clauses and non-defining relative clauses. You will often find them in this part of the Use of English paper.

EXAM EXERCISE 2

Robert Burns

1 was
2 do
3 the
4 little (**Note:** the word *unfortunately* makes it wrong to put *much* for the answer here)
5 after
6 by
7 short
8 be
9 them
10 an
11 gave (**Note:** the phrasal verb* *give up* means *to stop doing or thinking something*)
12 would (**Note:** the presence of *definitely* means that *might* or *could* are not possible)
13 of
14 had
15 which

A long-distance pigeon

EXAM EXERCISE 3

1 known
2 few
3 their
4 in **or** after
5 a
6 are
7 happened
8 been
9 where
10 off (**Note:** the phrasal verb* *set off* has the meaning of *leave* or *depart*)
11 was
12 who **or** that (**Note:** either *who* or *that* is possible as this is a defining relative clause: the words following explain who *the man* is, and this is important for a full understanding of the sentence. Compare with number **6** and **12** in Exam Exercise 1, and see Exam tip above.)
13 all (**Note:** *all the way* is a set expression which has the idea of a long distance)
14 than
15 on

Exam tip

In **1**, the phrase *known as* is used. Learn this phrase as it is very popular in this type of test. As an alternative, the word *called* is sometimes used, but this is not followed by *as* or by any other preposition.

Rhyming slang

EXAM EXERCISE 4

1 to
2 was
3 where
4 be
5 who
6 known
7 instead
8 a
9 one (**Note:** the answer must be *one* and not *some* because of the singular verb *is*, which comes a few words later)
10 which
11 do
12 unable (**Note:** as the reader has been told not to worry, the word here must suggest something negative about the ability of many cockneys to use rhyming slang)
13 even
14 so
15 of

Exam tip

In this part of the Use of English paper, as in Part 1, remember to read beyond the space before deciding on the answer – as in No. 9 above.

4 PART 3: TRANSFORMATIONS

In this part every question is worth **2 marks**.

There are two parts to every answer, each worth 1 mark. The two marks are separated by a plus sign (+). Therefore if the answer was written as

would like + *to leave*

you would get one mark for *would like* and one mark for *to leave*.

Where you see this mark / it means that two answers on both sides of the mark are possible. Therefore, if the answer was written as

would like / *would prefer* + *to leave*

you would gain the first mark for either *would like* or *would prefer*.

Where a word in the answer is in brackets, this means that the word may be used or may be missed out without changing the mark.

EXAM EXERCISE 1

1 had never watched television + before
2 was seen + by several
3 if I + liked
4 never seen + a bigger dog
5 how happy + Mary is
6 the only person + I can
7 I were you + I would / should
8 without + putting a stamp on
9 will be necessary + for her
10 such + an unpleasant man

EXAM EXERCISE 2

1 apologised + for breaking / for having broken
2 in case + he loses
3 cannot sing + as well as / so well as
4 took + them ten minutes to
5 in spite of + the noise
6 would go out + only if
7 did not remember / could not remember + anything
8 would rather + not
9 where they + had bought
10 less + friendly than

EXAM EXERCISE 3

1 was yesterday + when he / that he
2 (very) good + at speaking
3 were not + many (people) at
4 was shorter + than she had
5 of the heavy + rain
6 learnt to drive + in
7 was followed home + by
8 am not + as tall as / so tall as
9 was the only person + who / that
10 I had + met

Exam tip

Make sure you read the first sentence very carefully, and that you put all the necessary words into your answer. For example, in No 4 above, it would be easy to forget the word 'had', and so to write the wrong answer.

1 have not seen Paul + for
2 it be possible + for her
3 want anyone / anybody + to hear
4 had written + I could have
5 too heavy + for me to
6 sorry that + he had not
7 though + he was
8 did not see + anyone / anybody
9 to come to + a decision
10 (that) he + would be home

**EXAM
EXERCISE 4**

1 in case + it gets cold
2 their intention + to work
3 had seen + her boss
4 who + are not
5 was known + by / to
6 who was responsible + for breaking
7 were you + I would / should
8 lend you any money + unless
9 the birth + of
10 have eaten + so much

**EXAM
EXERCISE 5**

Exam tip

Remember, you must only use 5 words. In No. 6 above, it would be possible to say *who was responsible* + *for having broken*, but this is too many words, so it would be wrong.

1 even though + he has
2 if + she would take
3 since + we last went
4 if + you have
5 have any money + left
6 they + had just bought
7 I was short + of time
8 was + the first time
9 he had behaved + badly
10 mind not + leaving

**EXAM
EXERCISE 6**

5 PART 4: ERROR CORRECTION

All answers in this part of the paper are worth **1 mark**.

1 to (**Note:** *to* is never used immediately in front of *home*)
2 ✓
3 no
4 has (**Note:** this changes the main tense of the narrative*)
5 been (**Note:** *been* suggests the passive* voice so it would have to be *by his patients*, which would change the meaning)
6 to (**Note:** see the examples on page 28)

**PRACTICE
EXERCISE 1**

Answers and Notes

Exam tip

Double negatives* may not be used in English (see page 27). Look out for them as they are quite likely in this part of the Use of English paper.

PRACTICE EXERCISE 2

1 a (**Note:** *by train* is a set expression; the article *a* should not be used)
2 being (**Note:** *being* is not used with *ready*)
3 had (**Note:** *had* must refer to something which happened before he learnt to drive)
4 really (**Note:** *really* is in the wrong position; the correct position would be *She was not really keen on going to university*)
5 ✓
6 less (**Note:** *less* must have *than* after it)

PRACTICE EXERCISE 3

1 ✓
2 for (**Note:** *for* used after *send* changes the meaning: this would mean that the friends contacted the paper asking for a letter)
3 never (**Note:** a double negative; the sentence does not make sense if *nothing* is omitted)
4 for (**Note:** *in order to* is a set phrase; no other word must be put in it)
5 of (**Note:** the correct forms are *14 years old* and *14 years of age*)
6 himself (**Note:** when talking about *putting on* clothes, words such as *himself, herself, myself, yourself*, must not be used)

Exam tip

When there are two negatives in the line, be careful about deciding which is the extra one. Be sure the line makes sense when you take out one of the negatives, as in No. 3 above.

PRACTICE EXERCISE 4

1 which (**Note:** *which* must be followed by *was*: *which was selling*)
2 been (**Note:** *was been* is impossible; *had been* would be possible)
3 ✓
4 the (**Note:** *the* is not normally used after *plenty of*; if *the* were present here, it would refer to a specific type of wine)
5 being
6 of (**Note:** *all of the day* would be correct)

PRACTICE EXERCISE 5

1 of (**Note:** *few* can be followed by *of the*, but not by *of* alone)
2 going (**Note:** *going there* would be all right; *going here* does not make sense)
3 did (**Note:** *did* may not be followed by a past participle)
4 back (**Note:** *took my friend back home* would be correct
5 ✓
6 up (**Note:** we can say *come to a decision* or *come up with an idea; come up to* means *approach*)

A missing dog

00 one (**Note:** *on Saturday* means the most recent Saturday; *one Saturday* means a Saturday in the past; *on one Saturday* is impossible)

1 most (**Note:** *most* must be followed by *of*)

2 ✓

3 having (**Note:** the correct expression is either *for a cup of tea* or *to have a cup of tea*)

4 ✓

5 at

6 ✓

7 one (**Note:** *one* must be followed by *of*)

8 not (**Note:** *not* cannot be followed by a negative word (*nothing* in this sentence); we cannot take *nothing* out because *nothing of* is a fixed phrase)

9 might (**Note:** *might* cannot be used in front of *had*)

10 some (**Note:** *some* should be taken out; it seems to suggest that the writer is speaking about a group of dogs which she knows)

11 at

12 back

13 ✓

14 had (**Note:** *had* suggests that the people had felt annoyed with the lady before she brought the dog back)

15 a (**Note:** *a* is not used after *of* when followed by an abstract noun*)

A difficult journey

0 the

1 ✓

2 ✓

3 ✓

4 me (**Note:** when talking about putting on clothes, you do not use words such as *me*, *myself*, *him*, *himself*, *her*, *herself*)

5 too (**Note:** *too thick* must be followed by a phrase beginning with *for*, (e.g. *too thick for walking*)

6 my

7 very (**Note:** *very* cannot be used with *greatly*)

8 at

9 of (**Note:** although we say *quarter of an hour* and *three quarters of an hour*, we miss out *of* when speaking about *half an hour*)

10 to

11 had (**Note:** *had* suggests that the train arrived before the person was on the point of going back home)

12 yet (**Note:** the position of *yet* is wrong; *for yet another twenty minutes* would be correct)

13 ✓ (**Note:** you may possibly have thought that *on* was wrong in this sentence, but in fact it is perfectly acceptable; in front of a verb* which has the *-ing* ending, you may use either *keep* or *keep on*)

14 ✓

15 less (**Note:** *less* must be followed by *than*)

Exam tip

Look out for words that are extra just because they are in the wrong place, as in No. 12 above.

EXAM EXERCISE 3

An embarrassing experience

0 the (**Note:** *the last year* means the last year of a series, not the one which finished recently)
1 have (**Note:** *have a look* would be correct)
2 ✓
3 little (**Note:** *a little* would be correct, meaning *just after* or *shortly after*)
4 ✓
5 up (**Note:** with *high* the word *up* can refer only to a high position)
6 those (**Note:** *those* could be used only if the *traditional meals* had already been mentioned)
7 just (**Note:** *just* cannot be used in front of *well*)
8 has (**Note:** *has* changes the main narrative* tense* of the passage)
9 ✓
10 ✓
11 them (**Note:** *to them* would be correct)
12 hold (**Note:** the expression would have to be *get hold of*)
13 must
14 to (**Note:** the word *to* is not used in front of a noun* or pronoun* which follows the verb* *tell*)
15 ✓

EXAM EXERCISE 4

A visit to Stratford

0 of (**Note:** *few* can be followed by *of the* or by a noun*, but not by *of* alone)
1 have (**Note:** here *have booked* suggests that they have not yet stayed at the hotel but will be doing so in the future)
2 ✓
3 for
4 of (**Note:** *of* must be followed by *the*)
5 which (**Note:** *all* could be followed by *that* but not by *which*)
6 our (**Note:** if *bed* were in the plural, *our* would be correct)
7 by (**Note:** the expression being used is *to spend time / a day / an hour (etc.) doing something*)
8 each (**Note:** the set expression here is either *now and again* or *every now and again*)
9 ✓
10 at (**Note:** the verb *watch* is not followed by *at*; it is the verb *look* which is followed by *at*)
11 me
12 to (**Note:** when *rather* is used with *would*, meaning *prefer*, it must be followed immediately by the verb without the word *to*; *prefer* needs *to*: *I would rather go* but *I would prefer to go*)
13 ✓
14 had (**Note:** the tense* suggests that the writer recognised the woman before being in the pub)
15 then (**Note:** *then* is in the wrong place)

6 PART 5: WORD FORMATION

All answers in this part of the paper are worth **1 mark**.

You were asked to find two words for each of the words given. There are more than two words possible in many cases and so a longer list is given.

1 success   successful   successfully   unsuccessful   unsuccessfully
2 manager   management
3 translator   translation
4 displease   pleasure   displeasure   pleasant   unpleasant   pleasantly   unpleasantly
   pleasing
5 original   originally   unoriginal
6 considerable   considerably   consideration   considerate
7 following   follower
8 softly   soften
9 shopping   shopper   shopkeeper
10 believe   believable   unbelievable   believably   unbelievably

1 engineers   (*Both* and *brothers* indicate a plural)
2 extensions   (*several* indicates a plural)
3 impressions   (*were* indicates a plural)
4 difficulties   (*keep* instead of *keeps* indicates a plural)
5 cyclists   (*three of the* indicates a plural)
6 lawyers   (*think* instead of *thinks* indicates a plural)

1 improbable
2 irresponsible
3 unusual
4 disobey
5 illegally
6 uncertainty
7 unhelpful
8 incorrect
9 unlikely
10 disembark

1 unable
2 impossible
3 unwilling
4 disagrees
5 impatient
6 unsuitably
7 uninteresting
8 independent
9 careless
10 inconvenient

Answers and Notes

PRACTICE EXERCISE 1

1 baker
2 warmth
3 leadership
4 probably
5 preparations **(Note:** the word *are* indicates that *preparation* must be plural)
6 wonderful
7 kindness
8 safety
9 unfortunately **(Note:** as people would not be pleased if the film had almost finished when they arrived *unfortunately*, not *fortunately*, is needed here)
10 wealthy

PRACTICE EXERCISE 2

1 thirsty
2 sweeten
3 determination
4 generally
5 useless **(Note:** the words *old* and *now* indicate a negative idea about the washing machine)
6 resignation
7 seriously
8 inspectors
9 homeless
10 lucky **(Note:** it can be quite tempting to write *unlucky*, but the fact that she was *not* knocked down shows that in fact she was *lucky*)

PRACTICE EXERCISE 3

1 funny
2 tendency
3 unconscious
4 dangerous
5 individually
6 loneliness
7 stormy
8 organisations
9 insurance
10 qualifications **(Note:** *qualifications* must be plural because the article *an* is not in front of *extra*)

PRACTICE EXERCISE 4

1 strangers
2 widely
3 professional
4 responsibility
5 doubtful
6 considerably
7 treatment
8 artistic
9 undo
10 believes **(Note:** the noun *belief* is changed into the verb *believe* and the letter *s* is added as the subject* is singular: *Claire*)

62

A new shop

1 selection
2 energetic
3 fashionable
4 attractive
5 unfortunately
6 expensive
7 pleasure
8 helpful
9 advice (**Note:** note that you spell the verb* which is given *advise*, but the noun* which you have to form has the spelling *advice*)
10 succeed

A lion on the streets of London

1 peaceful
2 residents (**Note:** *a number of* indicates that *residents* must be plural)
3 length
4 scientist
5 eventually
6 dangerous
7 asleep (**Note:** *sleeping* may be tempting but you would not use this with *fast* as *fast asleep* is a set expression)
8 owner
9 unusual (**Note:** the meaning of the passage suggests a negative word)
10 neighbourhood

New jobs for Bridsea

1 improvement (**Note:** *a* in front of *large* means *improvement* cannot be plural)
2 expansion
3 decision
4 immediately
5 unlikely (**Note:** the presence of *although* and the fact that people should apply for jobs immediately, lead to the answer *unlikely* here)
6 production
7 successful
8 manager (**Note:** as we have a person's name, the answer must be *manager*, not *management*)
9 enthusiastic
10 contribution

Mobile phones

1 increasingly
2 sale
3 expensive
4 easily
5 useful (**Note:** *used* is not correct as the following word is *for*; *used by* would be correct)
6 impossible
7 annoying
8 peaceful
9 loudly
10 importance

TRIAL PAPER A

PART 1

The Number 13

1 D ambition
2 D understand
3 C meant
4 B fear (**Note:** *suffering* must be followed by *from*; *problem* must be followed by *with*; *anxiety* must be followed by *about*)
5 A any
6 B divided
7 C convinced
8 B produced (**Note:** *arrived* must be followed by *at*)
9 D lived (**Note:** *to live on* means *to continue living*; *to pass on* can mean *to die*)
10 A bother
11 D something (**Note:** *another* and *more* cannot be used with *else*)
12 A worry
13 C managed
14 D next
15 B safe

PART 2

From Baline to Berlin

16 so (**Note:** as an adjective and *that* come after the space, the word to go in the space must be *so*)
17 as
18 having
19 when
20 from
21 would
22 for (**Note:** the expression *if it had not been for* is a popular way of expressing the idea of something happening to prevent something worse occurring)
23 where
24 was
25 had
26 did
27 it
28 spite
29 was (**Note:** if you do not read the rest of the sentence, it is tempting to put *became* as the answer; however, the answer is *was* as the sentence speaks of how Irving Berlin was at the end of his life)
30 at

PART 3

31 he had + not missed
32 finds it difficult + to walk
33 were + more flowers
34 he would + be leaving
35 had replied + I would have
36 was responsible + for examining
37 can + be seen
38 had been able + to speak
39 did not have + (very) much
40 only shop + that was

An invitation

41 been
42 when
43 that
44 at (**Note:** distances do not have the word *at* in front of them)
45 be (**Note:** *be* would be correct in: *would be of interest to you*)
46 it
47 ✓
48 ✓
49 these (**Note:** *these* must refer to things which have already been mentioned, but no such things have been mentioned yet)
50 off (**Note:** *off* is never used with *bored*)
51 its (**Note:** the words *take place* are a set expression and there should be no other word between *take* and *place*.)
52 than (**Note:** *over* is never followed by *than; more than* would be correct)
53 coming
54 to (**Note:** *let* is never followed by *to*)
55 ✓

Fire at the station

PART 5

56 luckily
57 immediately
58 buildings (**Note:** as *the* is not in front of *other*, the following word must be plural)
59 injuries (**Note:** *were* indicates that *injury* must be plural)
60 service
61 operation
62 regional
63 investigation
64 impossible
65 certainty

TRIAL PAPER B

The Statue of Liberty

1 B stands
2 C short (**Note:** the presence of *just a* makes *long* and *far* unsuitable; *brief* is normally used only to refer to an amount of time)
3 B height
4 C date
5 A paid
6 D gift
7 D celebrate
8 B largely
9 C built
10 C pieces (**Note:** *to pull into pieces* is a set expression)
11 A most (**Note:** *most* is not used here to form a superlative* but it is used with the meaning of *very*)
12 A taking (**Note:** *going* must be followed by *on*)
13 B search (**Note:** *in search of* is a set expression)
14 D put up
15 A hope (**Note:** *faith* must be followed by *in;* the presence of *for the future* make *joy* and *success* unsuitable)

PART 2 ## Not telling the whole truth
16 a
17 when
18 whom
19 on (**Note:** the phrasal verb* *getting on* means *progressing*)
20 telling (**Note:** the verb to use with *lies* (and *the truth*) is *tell*)
21 had
22 was
23 lots **or** plenty **or** dozens
24 having **or** needing
25 little
26 live
27 about
28 did
29 them
30 more (**Note:** an adjective after *much* must be in the comparative*, which usually means *more*, or *less*, will come immediately after *much*)

PART 3
31 did not know + anybody / anyone
32 if / whether + he could / he might
33 for + having arrived
34 repaired the car + in
35 it had not been + foggy

36 a + better book
37 I would help + him
38 instead of + saving
39 is a year + since
40 if + we had not been

PART 4 ## A shopping trip
41 go (**Note:** *go and buy* would be correct)
42 on
43 the (**Note:** the set expression here is *at least* or *at the very least*)
44 have
45 ✓
46 more
47 ✓
48 to (**Note:** the verb* *to suit* is not followed by *to*)
49 had (**Note:** *had* makes it seem that the writer had bought a sandwich and tea in the café some time before)
50 to
51 found
52 long (**Note:** the word *long* should not be used with *over*; if you want a word to put with *over*, the most suitable one to use here would be *well: well over an hour*)
53 ✓
54 being
55 been

PART 5 ## Village football

56 impressive
57 annually
58 importance
59 inhabitants
60 encouragement
61 players

62 proudly
63 friendly (**Note:** *friendly* is an adjective, not an adverb, in spite of ending in *-ly*)
64 violence
65 professional

Appendix

This is a list of words which appear in the book marked with an asterisk (*). Each word is explained briefly, usually with examples. The explanations should help you understand these terms, but you should realise that they are simply for guidance and are not complete grammatical definitions of the words.

Adjectives
Adjectives are words which describe nouns* or pronouns*. The following words are adjectives:
clever   beautiful   long   old   green

Adverbs
Adverbs are words which describe verbs*, adjectives* and other adverbs. In English they often, but not always, end in the letters *-ly*. The following words are adverbs:
slowly   extremely   sadly   well   very

Articles
These are the short words that often come in front of nouns*: *a*, *an*, and *the*.

Auxiliary verbs
Auxiliary verbs are verbs* such as *have*, *had*, *will*, *would* which are used mainly to help form verb tenses*.

Comparative
This is the form of an adjective* or adverb* when two things are compared. The comparative is formed by putting *more* in front of the adjective or adverb. Often, instead of putting *more* in front of the adjective, *-er* is added to the end of the word:
'Smaller' is the comparative of 'small'.

Compound prepositions
Compound prepositions are prepositions* which consist of more than one word. Some examples are:
instead of   as well as   in front of   owing to   in addition to

Consonants
All letters, apart from **a**, **e**, **i**, **o** and **u** are known as consonants. (See vowels*.)

Indefinites
Indefinites are words which refer to people or things which are not clearly identified. Here are some examples.
any   some   anything   somebody   everywhere

Linking words
Linking words are words which join (or link) two parts of a sentence. The following are linking words:
and   because   which   as   when

Narrative
This is the story which is told in a passage.

Negatives
Negatives are words which, when added to a sentence, give a meaning of 'not'. The opposite of negative is positive.
Positive sentence: *He will leave tomorrow.*
Negative sentence: *He will not leave tomorrow.*
The most common negative word is *not*, but there are others, such as:
no   never   nobody   nowhere   nothing

Nouns
Nouns refer to people, animals, places, things. Some examples are:
teacher   cat   town   table   shop
Some nouns (which are known as abstract nouns) refer to qualities or states of mind. Some examples are:
happiness   skill   anger   peace   love

67

Object

The object of a sentence is the person, animal, place or thing which receives the action of the sentence. In the following sentence, *the man* is the object:
The dog bit the man.
(See also note on the passive voice*·)

Passive Voice

In the passive voice the subject receives the action of the sentence. (See notes on the subject* and the object*.) The following sentence is in the passive voice:
The man was bitten by the dog.

Phrasal verbs

Phrasal verbs are basically verbs* which gain new meanings when followed by certain prepositions*. There are hundreds of these verbs in English. Here are just a few examples:
take over   get by   keep up   make for   make out

Plural

Nouns* and pronouns* are in the plural when they refer to more than one. *Books* is the plural of *book*; *we* is the plural of *I*.

Prepositions

Prepositions are words which are used with nouns*, pronouns*, and sometimes verbs*, to link them with the rest of a sentence. Here are some examples:
of   by   to   through   without

Pronouns

Pronouns are words which replace nouns*. Here are some pronouns.
he   it   they   her   them
By using pronouns we do not have to keep repeating nouns; if we mention *the book* once, we do not need to keep saying *the book* every time we want to refer to it, we can say simply *it*.

Subject

The subject of a sentence is usually the person, animal, place or thing responsible for the action in a sentence. In the following sentence, *The dog* is the subject:
The dog bit the man.
(See also note on the passive voice*.)

Superlative

This is the form of an adjective* or adverb* which shows the most or least of a quality or quantity. The superlative is formed by putting *most* in front of the adjective or adverb. Often, instead of putting *most* in front of the adjective, *-est* is added to the end of the word:
'Tallest' is the superlative of 'tall'.

Tense

The tense of a verb* indicates when something happens, whether it is in the present, the past or the future.

Verbs

Verbs indicate actions, states of mind and possession. Some examples are:
run   think   own   speak   want

Vowels

The letters **a**, **e**, **i**, **o**, **u** are known as vowels.

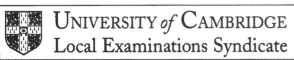
UNIVERSITY *of* CAMBRIDGE
Local Examinations Syndicate

SAMPLE

Examination Details	9999/03	99/D99
Examination Title	First Certificate in English	
Centre/Candidate No.	AA999/9999	
Candidate Name	A.N. EXAMPLE	

• Sign here if the details above are correct

☒

• Tell the Supervisor now if the details above
  are not correct

Candidate Answer Sheet: FCE Paper 3 Use of English

Use a pencil

For **Part 1**: Mark ONE letter for each question.

For example, if you think **C** is the
right answer to the question,
mark your answer sheet like this:

For **Parts 2, 3, 4** and **5**: Write your
answers in the spaces next to the
numbers like this:

0	*example*

Part 1				
1	A	B	C	D
2	A	B	C	D
3	A	B	C	D
4	A	B	C	D
5	A	B	C	D
6	A	B	C	D
7	A	B	C	D
8	A	B	C	D
9	A	B	C	D
10	A	B	C	D
11	A	B	C	D
12	A	B	C	D
13	A	B	C	D
14	A	B	C	D
15	A	B	C	D

Part 2	Do not write here
16	16
17	17
18	18
19	19
20	20
21	21
22	22
23	23
24	24
25	25
26	26
27	27
28	28
29	29
30	30

Turn over for Parts 3 - 5 →

SAMPLE

Part 3		Do not write here		
31		31 0 ☐	1 ☐	2 ☐
32		32 0 ☐	1 ☐	2 ☐
33		33 0 ☐	1 ☐	2 ☐
34		34 0 ☐	1 ☐	2 ☐
35		35 0 ☐	1 ☐	2 ☐
36		36 0 ☐	1 ☐	2 ☐
37		37 0 ☐	1 ☐	2 ☐
38		38 0 ☐	1 ☐	2 ☐
39		39 0 ☐	1 ☐	2 ☐
40		40 0 ☐	1 ☐	2 ☐

Part 4		Do not write here
41		☐ 41 ☐
42		☐ 42 ☐
43		☐ 43 ☐
44		☐ 44 ☐
45		☐ 45 ☐
46		☐ 46 ☐
47		☐ 47 ☐
48		☐ 48 ☐
49		☐ 49 ☐
50		☐ 50 ☐
51		☐ 51 ☐
52		☐ 52 ☐
53		☐ 53 ☐
54		☐ 54 ☐
55		☐ 55 ☐

Part 5		Do not write here
56		☐ 56 ☐
57		☐ 57 ☐
58		☐ 58 ☐
59		☐ 59 ☐
60		☐ 60 ☐
61		☐ 61 ☐
62		☐ 62 ☐
63		☐ 63 ☐
64		☐ 64 ☐
65		☐ 65 ☐

☐